WITH NAPOLEON IN RUSSIA

WITH NAPOLEON IN RUSSIA
The Illustrated Memoirs of Faber du Faur, 1812

EDITED AND TRANSLATED BY JONATHAN NORTH

Greenhill Books, London
Stackpole Books, Pennsylvania

With Napoleon in Russia
first published 2001 by Greenhill Books, Lionel Leventhal Limited, Park House, 1 Russell Gardens, London NW11 9NN
and
Stackpole Books, 5067 Ritter Road, Mechanicsburg, PA 17055, USA

British Library Cataloguing in Publication Data available
ISBN 1-85367-454-0
Library of Congress Cataloging-in-Publication Data available

Manufactured in China by Imago

Frontispiece:
On the road, not far from Pneva, 8 November 1812. See plate 76 for another version of this dramatic scene.

CONTENTS

FOREWORD

Christian Wilhelm von Faber du Faur is something of an enigmatic figure, yet his legacy is unique, startling and of immense historical value. He was an artist and a soldier, and his life was perhaps unexceptional until the year 1812 when, as a 32-year-old lieutenant in Napoleon's very grand army, he took part in the French Emperor's disastrous invasion of Russia. He marched with the main army, as part of the Kingdom of Württemberg's contingent, reached Moscow, survived the infamous retreat and witnessed the almost complete destruction of one of the finest military forces ever to take the field. And it is in his role as witness that Faber du Faur achieves his deserved place in history. For the German lieutenant took a sketchbook with him. Now preserved in superb condition in the Anne S. K. Brown Military Collection in Rhode Island, this loosely bound volume is a priceless record of the terrible events of 1812 and records scenes, in pencil, ink and watercolour, on an almost daily basis. Nothing seems to have escaped the eye of the artist – Russian peasant, burning church, shaded glade or the aftermath of a bloody battle – and the sketches, drawn between marches, at camp or in the ruins of Smolensk or Moscow, offer us, for the very first time, a visual history of the progress of a military campaign.

The sketches were later drawn up and published as plates, many of them hand-coloured, and Faber du Faur, along with a fellow survivor of the Russian campaign, von Kausler, added textual commentary and reminiscences to provide a brilliant and complete record of the fateful invasion. However, the text is an accompaniment, as the true value of the record lies in the images and their unique, moving, touching and disturbing ability to bring home what it was like to march with Napoleon to Moscow, witness the death of half a million men and endure the rigours of that infernal winter of 1812.

Born in Stuttgart on 18 August 1780, Faber du Faur grew up in the rather provincial atmosphere of the capital of Württemberg and spent most of his life there. The Faber du Faurs were of French origin, not Huguenots as is sometimes suggested but Armagnac rebels exiled from France in the fifteenth century who settled in southern Germany. Christian Wilhelm's family was eminently military, his father, Albrecht Achilles von Faber du Faur, serving in the Württemberg armed forces, achieving the rank of *Reiteroberst*; his mother, Philippa Frederika Zoller, was the daughter of a lecturer at the military academy. Christian Wilhelm had a brother and a sister, but his mother died when he was three, in 1783, and his father took a new wife shortly afterwards, marrying Christiane Kluepfel.

Christian Wilhelm was sent to grammar school and then trained as a lawyer, although evidently he had more of a talent for illustration – a series of playing cards with scenes from Schiller's play *Wallenstein* were illustrated by him and published in Cotta in 1807 – but he followed his father's footsteps and entered the army of the newly created Kingdom of Württemberg in 1809. He was in the artillery in the 1809 campaign against Austria and again in the invasion of Russia as part of Württemberg's contingent, serving in the 2nd Foot Artillery Battery. He was awarded the Legion of Honour for his actions during the battle for Smolensk in August 1812 and, later, the Knight's Cross. He was one of only 100 Württembergers (22 from the artillery) to return to Poland in December 1812, and these men, the remnant of 15,000, gathered at Inovratslav on 8 January 1813.

Having survived the catastrophic retreat of the French army from Moscow, he was promoted to captain, re-joined Napoleon's forces in the spring of 1813 and fought at Bautzen, being badly wounded during the battle. He spent the rest of 1813 and much of 1814 recuperating, and, whilst recovering from his wounds in Ludwigsburg, in March 1814, he married Maria Margaretta Bonavenuta von Hirlinger. In 1815 he joined the Württemberg contingent that was mobilising to fight Napoleon;

these troops saw little action as the campaign was of short duration – the French Emperor was defeated at Waterloo and peace was again restored. Faber du Faur, however, persevered with his military career and became a major in 1819, a lieutenant-colonel in 1836, a colonel in 1840 and a general in 1849, serving Württemberg's army faithfully and advising on the rebuilding of Ulm and on Frankfurt's fortifications.

Christian Wilhelm's sketches of the Russian campaign were first exhibited in 1816, but in 1827 the Augsburg publisher Christian Autenrieth offered to publish a series of plates of scenes from 1812. Between 1827 and 1830 the sketches were drawn up and coloured and, in 1831, began to be offered for sale. A small number of bound collections of plates were produced, diplomatically dedicated to the Crown Prince of Württemberg and entitled *Pictures from my Portfolio, Collected in situ during the 1812 Campaign in Russia*. A French- and German-language text was later provided to accompany the plates, the German version being largely written in verse. One of these special large-format, presentation editions can be found in the Anne S. K. Brown Military Collection, along with the considerably more modest sketchbook.

Faber du Faur retired from the army in October 1851, receiving a pension of 2,160 guilders. He died in Stuttgart on 6 February 1857, being buried with his wife Maria, who had died in 1846. Their son, Otto, was born in 1828 and also served in the army before renouncing his military career in 1866, concentrating on painting and studying under Delacroix in Paris.

Frederich von Kausler, who collaborated with Faber du Faur on the text, was also an officer in Württemberg service. In the 1812 campaign he served as a lieutenant in the artillery, acting as a staff officer attached to III Corps' headquarters and winning the Knight's Cross, and he later rose to the rank of colonel. Like Faber du Faur's, his career revolved around the military and he achieved some reputation as a historian, publishing a detailed military atlas in 1839.

Whilst there have been many accounts of Napoleon's invasion of Russia – penned by honest soldiers, gallant adventurers or face-saving generals – this exceptional record of the trials and tribulations wrought by one of history's greatest catastrophes is unsurpassed in its detail, honesty and humanity.

Jonathan North
London 2001

INTRODUCTION: NAPOLEON'S CAMPAIGN IN RUSSIA

At 11 o'clock in the evening of 23 June 1812 Morand's division of I Corps marched over the river Niemen by means of three pontoon bridges and set foot on Russian soil. Napoleon's invasion of Russia had begun. For this massive undertaking an enormous force had been assembled, drawn from every corner of Europe. Faber du Faur was one of 450,000 men to march into Russia, and Napoleon could call upon reserves and supports on either flank, elements which boosted this total to 600,000 men and 250,000 horses. Although the majority of these men were French, or at least serving in French uniform, a large proportion were furnished by vassals and allies. Thus there were Italians (24,000), Neapolitans (6,000), Poles (65,000), Bavarians (32,000), Badeners (5,000), Westphalians (27,000), Saxons (12,000), Faber du Faur and his fellow Württembergers (15,000), troops from smaller German states (15,000), troops from the Balkans (4,000), Spaniards (3,000) and Portuguese (4,000). The French had even secured Prussian cooperation and a contingent covered the Grande Armée's northern flank. A similar treaty with Austria had been concluded, Napoleon's father-in-law, the Emperor Francis, providing 40,000 men for operations in the Ukraine.

Napoleon's army was one of the most imposing military hosts ever to take the field, and considerable effort had gone into uniforming, equipping and training. The Imperial Guard and I Corps were particularly magnificent, but other formations could also boast fine troops. Count Bourgoing of the Young Guard describes some of Marshal Ney's corps:

'I studied with awe and respect the French line regiments in III Corps. There were no youthful faces here, unlike in our Tirailleurs, for these men bore the martial aspect of veterans.'

Alexander I of Russia learned of the invasion on the 24th. He and his generals had concentrated all available troops on the border with Poland, Barclay de Tolly commanding the First Army of 120,000 troops and Bagration leading the Second Army of some 40,000 men. The command structure was not unified, which led to confusion, as did interference by Alexander himself, and in the first few days of the campaign the Russians beat a hasty retreat. Barclay fell back towards Drissa, whilst Bagration did his best to elude the French, cover Minsk and prepare to join up with Barclay. Russian headquarters was amazed at the scale of the invading host, for the Russian armies in Lithuania and the Ukraine only amounted to half as many men.

Napoleon's offensive was quick and aggressive in those long, hot summer days as his troops were enthusiastic to quit a devastated Poland and get to grips with the enemy. Kovno was occupied, and there followed an immediate push for Vilna with the Reserve Cavalry, I Corps and the Imperial Guard. A symbolic victory was gained when the French entered Vilna on 28 June. The French pushed forwards, seeking to locate and destroy Russian concentrations. Fortunately for the Russians, on 29 June, massive rainstorms swept Lithuania and turned the roads into morasses of slippery mud. Ney noted the consequences of the storms in a letter to Berthier on 30 June: 'The rain, which hasn't stopped falling in torrents for the last twelve hours, means that it is impossible for the Army Corps to march along anything other than main roads.' Despite this, Napoleon single-mindedly pushed his troops, and those on his flanks, to get forward, trap and defeat Barclay and Bagration in detail and finish the campaign in a decisive battle.

As the French advanced, exhausted by forced marches and muddy conditions, and – as so well described by Faber du Faur in his commentary to Plate 4 – with their draught horses dying by the thousands, they found themselves in territory devoid of supplies. Both Germany and Poland had suffered from the passage of troops, but Lithuania was very quickly stripped to the bone. The province had supported 150,000 Russians for the last three months, and any supplies not being used up then were now burnt by the retreating Russians or rapidly pillaged or destroyed by bands of marauders. Marauding had been a problem right from the start of the campaign as men like those depicted by Faber du Faur in Plates 3 and 8 combed Lithuania for food, sparing nothing, pitying nobody. Captain Skeplicki of the Polish Guard Lancers noted the effect of such disorganisation in a report to General Krasinski:

'It is my duty to inform you, general, that the terrible behaviour of the stragglers is making a bad impression on the inhabitants. I have seen with my own eyes the village of Dousniatoui pillaged by our cuirassiers. They wander around in groups of four, five or six and fear of them has driven the people into the forests.'

Many commanders sought to put an end to marauding's evil influence on discipline and military operations. Marshal Ney was one such officer, writing on 5 July that 'I have sought to restore a measure of discipline. Men found to be carrying stolen objects will be sent before courts-martial. Several have already been shot and I expect their example to produce the required effect.' Yet some commanders persisted in turning a blind eye to the looting, putting it down to the fortunes of war or excusing it as the soldiers' recompense for not having received any food, money or supplies.

The army's own supplies were far to the rear, loaded on to slow-moving wagons. Even the normally well-off Imperial Guard was suffering, General Roguet noting, on 30 June, that his troops had 'not had a bread ration for the last three days'. The rigours of such a campaign, combined with the arduous forced marches, proved too much for many of the thousands of young troops in Napoleon's army; Heinrich von Brandt, whose regiment was marching behind the Young Guard, noted that the newly-raised regiments 'were trailing stragglers, who could be seen stretched out along the sides of the road, mixed up with the dead horses'.

Although many bore the tribulations with equanimity, others sought the first opportunity to desert – the Bavarians, in particular, were described as having 'a mania for desertion' – and hundreds of reluctant conscripts made off into the endless forests or were caught by imperial gendarmes sweeping behind the army. The French army contained an entire division of reformed deserters (32nd Division, XI Corps) and many line regiments had had to absorb such transgressors in the build-up to war, as Marshal Berthier noted to Napoleon in February 1812:

'Sire, the Minister of War has acquainted me with your order, dated 6 February, that 721 deserters, condemned to hard labour, be pardoned and sent on to Wesel. Here they shall be armed and equipped and sent to join the corps currently in Germany. I have the honour of suggesting that these 721 men be assigned to the 4th, 18th and 72nd Line and the 11th Light, which form part of the II Corps of the Observation of the Elbe. These four regiments are the only French regiments in this corps not to have yet received such deserters.'

Napoleon, now directing operations from the Bishop's Palace in Vilna, continued to put pressure the Russians as they withdrew methodically and in good order. Murat was amazed: 'You have no idea of how the Russians are retreating: they leave nothing, absolutely nothing, behind.' Davout, supported by Napoleon's brother Jerome, harried Bagration, and, marching 400 kilometres in just two weeks, pushed the Russian general's troops through Minsk, seizing a considerable Russian depot to the relief of his own troops. But still the Russians were slipping away, and it seemed increasingly difficult for the French to ascertain exactly where the Russians were and what they intended to do.

Less than a month into the campaign, the Grande Armée was suffering intensely. Difficulties for the whole army increased as the advance continued, a Württemberg officer in III Corps noting that 'food is bad and insufficient. Sickness is rife and augmented by the heat of the day and coldness of the night.' Statistics reported from the French hospital in Glubkoi on 27 July bear out the fact that sickness was the prime cause of most of the Grande Armée's casualties thus far into the campaign: of 1,006 occupants, 864 were suffering from 'fever', 110 had been wounded in battle, fourteen had venereal disease and eighteen were described as having scurvy.

Despite such problems, the pursuit of the Russians continued without relaxation. The Russians, now more confident in their movements since the departure of the Czar for St Petersburg on 16 July, did rally at Vitebsk towards the end of July, after shaking off the pursuing French cavalry at Ostrovno, but then continued to Smolensk and gave every sign that they intended to defend this ancient city with the combined armies of Barclay and Bagration. Their army had suffered considerably during its retreat from Vilna to Smolensk: some 30,000 men had disappeared from the ranks – some had been killed in battle, others had deserted and still more had fallen sick and been evacuated to hospital.

At Vitebsk, which went up in flames shortly after the arrival of the French, Napoleon, sensing the exhaustion of his own troops, and impending battle, allowed the forward elements of the French army a few days of much needed rest. A month of campaigning had not brought the decisive result Napoleon desired. Hoping that the Russians might now offer battle in defence of Smolensk, he gathered his troops for the decisive encounter – screened by a jaded cavalry – and promised them winter quarters in the conquered city.

Napoleon advanced out of Vitebsk on the 14th, his cavalry encountering a division under Neverovskii and pushing it back after a bloody encounter. After a half-hearted celebration of the imperial birthday, Napoleon arrived outside the walls of Smolensk in the humid afternoon of 16 August. His army showed signs of the considerable stress and hardship it had undergone. Losses during the advance had been enormous, and much of the army had wasted away. The fine Württemberg contingent of III Corps had numbered 170 officers and 7,624 men on 1 July; on 15 August it had shrunk to a mere 146 officers and 3,462 men. Other corps showed similar losses, only the Old Guard having come thus far relatively intact. Even so, the French army was eager for battle and looked forward to contesting possession of Smolensk.

The Russians left a rearguard of 13,000 men under the determined Rayevski to defend the city and cover their withdrawal. The French and Russians fought a bloody battle in the evening of the 16th, and the Russians, now under Dokhturov, suffered heavily. Barclay, nervous at being cut off from Moscow, and fearing that a combined army of 105,000 men was insufficient to confront Napoleon's forces, had ordered the complete evacuation of the city on the night of the 16th. Bagration was despatched at dawn on the 17th to cover the Russian retreat eastwards, and Barclay now determined to pull his entire command out of the city. The French launched a series of bloody assaults that day, supporting their attacks with massed artillery and setting the town on fire – a scene captured brilliantly by Faber du Faur. Their troops pushed into the suburbs that night, fighting a running battle, but their progress was arrested by the burning of the city's bridges. Meanwhile, the Russians evacuated Smolensk. The following morning, Ney's corps again bore the brunt of the French pursuit – the Württembergers once again finding themselves in the front line – fighting a series of actions against Korf and Tutchkov. One such action at Valutina Gora developed into a determined fight, the French pouring in Gudin's division in support of Ney and the Russians bringing their artillery to bear. Unfortunately General Junot, commanding VIII Corps, coming up from the south, failed to exploit an opportunity to take the Russians in the rear and, towards nightfall on the 18th, the Russians disengaged and resumed their trek eastwards. Casualties on both sides had been heavy. The 25th Division had lost some 25 officers and 1,116 men killed and wounded, and was now barely the strength of a small brigade.

Pushing aside appeals – many of which were subsequently invented – to halt and winter at Smolensk, Napoleon still sought a decisive encounter and urged his troops on over the traditional boundary between Lithuania and Russia.

To the north, Napoleon's Prussian allies, and a small Polish/German division, commanded by Marshal Macdonald, trundled over the Niemen, planning to lay siege to Riga. II and VI Corps, under Oudinot and St Cyr, marched roughly parallel with the Grande Armée's advance. In August they fought an indecisive battle with Wittgenstein's Russians at Polotsk. To the south, the Austrians and Saxons of Schwarzenberg swept into the western Ukraine, playing cat-and-mouse with Tormassov's Russians. Tormassov eagerly awaited news of the Russian Army of the Danube, 35,000 men under Admiral Chichagov, which was slowly marching northwards after Russia had hastily concluded peace with the Turks in May.

Napoleon's army continued to harry the Russians. Davout and Murat – squabbling and frustrated – led the advance. On the 29th the French received news that Barclay had been superseded by General Kutusov. This, Napoleon believed, was a sure sign that the Russians would now offer battle. The crafty Kutusov, popular with the Russian soldiers and the Russian nobility, sought hard for a suitable position to fight a defensive battle and eventually resolved to make a stand close by the little village of Borodino.

The Russians took up positions among the small hills and steep gullies that characterised the area. Their right flank was anchored on the river Kolotscha, their left protected by the thick forests around Utitza. To support their centre, placed largely on the heights to the south of Borodino village, the Russians built a series of earthworks bolstered by wood hewn from the forest-like terrain – the most famous of which was dubbed the 'Grand Redoubt'. Kutuzov had received reinforcements, mostly militiamen under Miloradovich and Markov, and believed that the governor of Moscow would be sending him more. In all, Russia deployed 120,000 men and 640 guns to bar Napoleon's way to Moscow.

Napoleon concentrated at Gjatsk. His troops advanced on 4 September, skirmishing constantly with the Russian rearguard. On the 5th, Murat felt his way along the Russian position and reported that the Russians were making a stand. That afternoon the French stormed Kutuzov's most advanced position – the Schevardino redoubt. Napoleon spent the next day on reconnaissance, hurrying forward as many troops as he could. By the evening of the 6th, 128,000 French and allies, with 580 guns, settled down before the Russian positions, waiting for the order to attack. A Württemberg cavalry officer summed up the thoughts and fears of the entire French army:

'We'd seen the Russian position and it was good, and we saw their entrenchments and, behind them, masses of troops, their weapons shining in the sun.

'We were convinced that our army was superior in numbers and that we were better acquainted with the practice of war. But we knew that the Russians were steady, and fought obstinately even against canister.'

The French artillery began firing through the morning haze at 6 o'clock. As the bombardment continued, Napoleon sent Ney, Davout and Eugène against the Russian positions whilst Poniatowski advanced against the Russian left. The advance in the centre and against Borodino degenerated into ferocious close-quarter fighting as both sides fed more and more men into the struggle. Infantry attacked, cavalry counter-attacked, and artillery swept the field and reduced columns of men to bloody ribbons. Eugène took Borodino village and Ney managed to storm the fleches to the south of Semenovskaya village – only to lose them to a counter-attack by Bagavout.

Poniatowski's attack on the Russian left led to the Poles' seizing Utitza but being unable to make any further impression against Tutchkov. On the Russian right, Kutuzov agreed to send Platov and Uvarov on a flanking attack just as the French were absorbed by the drama around Borodino and the Grand Redoubt. The Russian horsemen were beaten off by Delzons' French and Croatian infantry, but not before sowing some apprehension and confusion on the French left: the attack had alarmed Eugène and gained an hour's respite for the Russian centre.

As the Russian horsemen rode back to their lines, the French made a final convulsive effort to capture the Russian centre, pouring in Broussier's infantry and Caulaincourt's cavalry. The Russians, exhausted and choked by the billowing smoke blowing into their faces, were sabred and bayoneted where they stood. Russian reserves counter-attacked with the bayonet but were mown down by the French artillery. As the Russians seemed at breaking point, with all their reserves committed, Napoleon was urged to consider an attack by his Imperial Guard – 25,000 fresh troops poised for victory. He decided against a final attack, claiming that he could not use his Guard so far from home, and directed his artillery to increase its fire and thus drive the Russians back. Late that evening, the

Russians pulled back to Mozhaisk, taking as many of their wounded as they could.

Dead and wounded littered the battlefield, as Faber du Faur shows in his haunting portrait of Borodino's aftermath. Napoleon's army suffered 40,000 casualties (including 49 generals), whilst the Russians lost 47,000. Leaving to Junot's corps the unenviable task of clearing the field, Napoleon continued the advance towards Moscow, which was some 70 miles away. Covering this ground took the French a week. A fierce struggle for Mojaisk, on the 9th, resulted in the French capture of that town, along with 10,000 unfortunate wounded Russians. On the 13th Kutuzov conferred with his generals and, contrary to their opinion that Moscow should not be given up without a further battle, put the welfare of his army first and retreated towards Kaluga in the south, marching via Kolomna. Moscow was evacuated during the 13th and 14th, and when the French arrived before the gates they found the city largely deserted but for Russian wounded, prisoners released from the jails, foreign nationals and a handful of inhabitants.

Then, in the evening of the 15th, fire swept the city. It burned throughout that night and the following day. Moscow's wooden buildings were soon ablaze as the fire, fanned by strong winds, took hold. Not only did wooden buildings suffer, but out of 2,570 brick buildings only 578 survived the conflagration, the rest being completely gutted. Although parts of the city remained untouched, including the Kremlin, most of Moscow was reduced to a pile of ash.

Meanwhile the Russian war against Napoleon's long line of communications began in earnest. Convoys were attacked by bands of partisans and peasants, Cossacks pounced on small detachments, couriers were intercepted and isolated garrisons were overwhelmed. Napoleon, sensing an impossible situation, strove hard to make Alexander negotiate, sending Lauriston to Kutuzov to present peace proposals. Alexander, his firmness overcoming his natural irresolution, refused to countenance peace with Napoleon. Lauriston was turned back and the army began to buzz with rumours of retreat. On the 14th orders were issued to stop artillery from proceeding beyond Smolensk. On the 16th preparations were made for the wounded to be evacuated from Moscow and orders were issued to the commissaries to gather stores of warm clothing in Smolensk. All indications suggest that Napoleon was going to abandon Moscow towards the end of October; bad news, however, precipitated the departure.

Murat had shadowed Kutuzov's rearguard, and fought in a number of actions along the Tchernitskaja, and then placed himself before the Russian's partially fortified camp at Tarutino. Despite an unofficial truce, there was some skirmishing, but, on 18 October, the Russians under Bennigsen attacked in force, initially taking the French by surprise before being themselves driven back.

News of Tarutino arrived whilst Napoleon was reviewing III Corps. The Tarutino episode, and the loss of 36 guns, stung Napoleon into action. Leaving Mortier with a rearguard in the Kremlin – with orders to blow it up – the Grande Armée, followed by a huge caravan of vehicles and camp followers, marched off to the south-west in sombre procession. On 21 October the Kremlin was partially blown up, and explosions continued until the 23rd.

The French marched towards Kaluga. An encounter battle flared up at Malojaroslavets on the 23rd, Prince Eugène, Napoleon's son-in-law, being attacked by Dokhturov and both sides feeding in reinforcements until the French and Italians drove the Russians, now under Kutuzov's own command, from the town. Kutuzov's Russians withdrew and took up a strong position two miles away, seemingly ready to fight every step of the way, but in fact themselves preparing to continue the withdrawal. Napoleon and his marshals, fearing another Borodino, altered course and marched for Mozhaisk and the old Moscow–Smolensk road. The retreat had begun.

The Russians, sensing victory at last, but still wary of Napoleon, sent Cossacks forward to harass the French whilst their main body shadowed the enemy to the south-east, hoping for an opportunity to detach elements from the imperial column, isolate them and defeat them in detail. On 3 November the Russians, under Miloradovich, attempted just this near Viasma, directing troops against the gap between Eugène and Davout's rearguard. The Russians were beaten off and they fell back to their menacing positions to the south. On 4 November snow began to fall. The French, and many of the Russians, found themselves unprepared. Their clothing was light and their horses were not shod for ice. Spirits dropped and casualties mounted in the French army. Wagons and guns were burnt or abandoned, troops threw down their weapons and the imperial army was increasingly shepherded along a road strewn with their own dead and dying.

Meanwhile, way to the south, the Russians under Chichagov and Sacken were outmanoeuvring Schwarzenberg. To the north, Wittgenstein, reinforced by troops from Finland, began to exert pressure against II and VI Corps on Napoleon's northern flank. An inconclusive battle was again fought at Polotsk, where II Corps' Swiss troops distinguished themselves, on 19 October, but the French pulled back to Glubokoi (VI Corps), to cover Vilna, and Tchasniki (II Corps), to link up with Victor's IX Corps. There was some manoeuvring, but, on 7 November, a grave blow was struck when Vitebsk fell to the Russians. Napoleon learnt of this setback when, on 9 November, he entered Smolensk with his Guard.

Smolensk, from the start, was a disappointment. There were insufficient supplies, and those that were available were poorly distributed – the Imperial Guard getting the most and leaving precious few for the rearguard. Smolensk's administration had been sadly lacking and the reserves and reinforcements gathered there were totally dispirited by the appearance of the mass of fugitives that had once been the Grande Armée. The retreat would have to continue. It began again on the 12th, with Junot and the dismounted cavalry pushing ahead towards Orsha. Napoleon and the Guard left on the 14th, Eugène on the 15th. Davout and Ney, now acting as the rearguard, left on the 16th, bickering and sullen. The Russians, instead of attacking Smolensk, had, however, skirted round the city and were preparing for another attempt to intercept the French. On the 16th Miloradovich's men attacked near Krasnoi, cutting off Davout and Ney and bruising Eugène in the process. On the 17th, Napoleon turned back to assist Davout and Ney, who had still not left Smolensk. Davout slipped through the Russians, urging Ney forward, but III Corps, having found the Russians barring his way, turned into the woods and attempted to cross the Dnepr. After a series of running battles, characterised by desperate fighting in the incredible cold, Ney rejoined the army with just 500 men – all that remained of III Corps.

The foiling of Kutuzov's plan and the dramatic escape of Ney, the bravest of the brave, raised morale in the French army, as did the numerous supplies gathered at Orsha. But hope was soon shattered by ugly rumours of the surrender of Minsk – a key French base, full of essential supplies – and the news that the Russians of Chichagov were advancing to cut the French line of retreat at the Beresina. The bridge at Borisov assumed tremendous importance, threatened now as it was by Russians advancing from the south and Wittgenstein's Russians pushing Victor down from the north.

Chichagov had taken Minsk on 17 November and hurried northwards to the Beresina with his 35,000 veterans. On the 21st his vanguard defeated a weak French garrison commanded by Dombrowski defending the Borisov bridge. The Russians drove the French and Poles over the bridge and out through the little town of Borisov. Oudinot counter-attacked and swept into the town but was unable to secure the bridge – the only one over the Beresina – which the Russians burnt as they withdrew.

At Toloczin Napoleon heard that Minsk had definitely fallen, and at Bobr news came that the Borisov bridge had been taken by Chichagov. On the morning of the 25th the Emperor was told that the Borisov bridge had been destroyed, but Oudinot then reported that his light cavalry, under Corbineau, had discovered a ford near Studianka, and the marshal decided to use this ford as a crossing point, although the water was 1.5 metres deep and the river had widened owing to a recent thaw. Napoleon despatched General Eblé and Chasseloup to aid Oudinot's artillery and engineers in constructing bridges. A detachment of Oudinot's troops made a demonstration to the south of Borisov, hoping to draw the Russians away from the scene of the impending action. To the surprise of all the ruse worked, and Chichagov, starved of information as to the exact whereabouts of both Napoleon's and Kutuzov's armies, headed south, leaving just Langeron opposite Borisov and a screen of Cossacks opposite Studianka. Eblé could now throw himself into the task of constructing two bridges. Studianka was virtually demolished for wood and Eblé, who had destroyed the bridging train at Orsha saving only two wagons with essential tools, began work during the night of 25/26 November. His gallant pontonniers – some of whom were Dutch and some Sailors of the Imperial Guard – worked shoulder-deep in freezing water, but, by noon the next day, two 100-metre-long bridges, one for infantry and cavalry and the other for vehicles and artillery, had been constructed.

Oudinot and Dombrowski were the first to cross, and they secured a series of bridges which took the Vilna road over treacherous marshes around Zembin. As Oudinot was crossing, the main army dragged its weary way from Borisov to the crossing point. Victor's three divisions of IX Corps took over rearguard duties from Davout and prepared to face Wittgenstein, and Platov and Yermolov were sent on ahead from Kutuzov's main army. The Russians were suffering, too, from lack of supplies and from the harsh weather.

Throughout 27 November Ney and elements of the Young Guard crossed over to the right bank. Brandt, in Claparède's division, describes the crossing:

'It had stopped snowing, the cold had eased off slightly and it promised to be a fine day. It must have been around ten o'clock when our division, deployed in columns, began to cross the Beresina. The planks of the bridge were by no means even, and when we crossed some of the planks were already missing, especially as we drew closer to the far bank. There the entire bridge was below the water level and we had water up to our ankles.'

With Victor's relatively fresh troops acting as rearguard, Napoleon sent his Guard over the river followed by Junot, Eugène and Davout. The Emperor himself crossed the Beresina, escorted by 200 Chasseurs à Cheval, later that afternoon. Between the units numbers of stragglers made their way over to the far side of the river even though gendarmes were posted on the left bank to ensure that only armed men were allowed across. A mass of weary stragglers had, however, encamped at the approaches to the bridge, blocking access and choking the movement of troops. They huddled around flickering campfires as the temperatures dropped. It was an exceptionally cold night.

As dawn broke, Chichagov, realising his mistake, made his way northwards to Borisov and sent Langeron forward. Langeron was beaten back by Ney, and Chichagov made preparations for an all-out attack.

At 9.00 a.m. the first wave of the Russian assault, consisting of seven regiments of Jägers supported by artillery, made its way forward through the snow and partially wooded and broken terrain and opened a heavy fire on the French position. Oudinot's Swiss kept the Russians back by repeated bayonet charges until being forced back in turn by deadly Russian artillery. The French then launched a counter-attack, spearheaded by Doumerc's cuirassier division, and seized the initiative, launching an infantry attack in support. The Russians, unable to stand the pressure, were beaten back, thus allowing the Grande Armée to continue its march towards Vilna.

Whilst the bitter battle swung first this way and then that, the terrible ordeal of crossing the river continued. Jostled, crushed, pushed and shoved, crowds of fugitives streamed across the river, spurred on by panic and fear of Wittgenstein's guns – guns that were now in range of the bridges – for Victor was being steadily pushed back and lost his rearguard, commanded by Partonneaux, in confused fighting along the Borisov road. At 6.00 p.m., after it had already been dark for two hours, fighting died down before ceasing altogether.

That night, lit by a bright moonlight sky, Victor's corps began withdrawing, pushing its way towards the bridge, and began crossing in good order at 9.00 p.m. They left 20,000 stragglers huddled around the flickering fires; worn out and inert, they awaited the morning.

Eblé had orders to destroy the bridges the next morning but he delayed as long as possible to give the non-combatants a final chance to cross. Then, being unable to risk the bridges falling into Russian hands, he ordered Seruzier to fire them at 9.00 a.m. An anguished howl went up as their only means of escape vanished in flames. The majority would die of hunger or of cold, but a vast number would die of typhus, which swept the little town of Borisov over the next few weeks.

The French, turning their backs on the disaster, pressed on towards Vilna. Their troubles were not over. Vilna was still some distance away. The march from the Beresina to Vilna was desperate. The cold had grown more intense, and morale and discipline had collapsed altogether. The instinct for self-preservation, in all its brute selfishness, now, more than ever, came to the fore.

All eyes looked to Vilna for respite, but, before it was reached, Napoleon quit his army. He would head for Paris to prepare for the next campaign, negate the impact of bad news from the east and rouse his tardy government. Command of the army passed to Murat, and it was the cavalryman who led what little remained of it into Vilna on 9 December. It quickly became apparent that, contrary to Napoleon's expectations, he would not be able to hold the city. The French abandoned Vilna on the 10th, what little remaining of VI Corps acting as rearguard. The Russians came on slowly, for they too were exhausted.

As the French retreat continued, hasty orders went out to Macdonald and Schwarzenberg to pull back over the Niemen – something the main body did on the 13th, passing through Kovno and crossing the Russian frontier into the Grand Duchy of Warsaw.

As Macdonald was withdrawing, his Prussian contingent hesitated and was overtaken by the Russians. The Prussians quickly signed a convention, which effectively made it clear that their divisions had defected.

Murat, learning of the convention, appointed Eugène commander of the army and withdrew to Naples. Eugène threw most of the survivors into fortresses along the Vistula. Most of these would be besieged the next year, their garrisons either dying from disease or surrendering to the victorious Allies.

Casualties had been horrific. Eugène was able to gather some 30,000 survivors, some 10,000 were thrown into Danzig, and perhaps 60,000 (largely unreliable) Austrians, Poles and Saxons remained to cover Warsaw. These, and the few thousands wounded and sick that had been evacuated during the campaign, were all that remained of both the mighty host that had crossed the Niemen and the troops subsequently despatched in support. Of course many thousands had deserted and made their way quietly back to their homelands, but, even so, the vast majority had perished or fallen into the hands of the Russians. I, II, III and IV Corps combined numbered just 6,400 infantry in February 1813. The Old Guard could field just 500, with another 800 in hospital. Napoleon's allies and vassals had suffered tremendously,

even those that had not gone as far as Moscow. The Bavarian VI Corps crossed the Niemen into Poland some 300 men strong, having lost 28,700 men in the course of the campaign. Although the four Italian infantry regiments, serving as part of IV Corps, had not fought at Borodino, they counted just 309 officers and men in January 1813, the demoralised survivors of nearly 10,000 fine troops.

Although a number of stragglers and sick later re-joined the remnants of the Grande Armée, it is estimated that the French lost nearly 450,000 soldiers, killed or made prisoner during the campaign. This astonishing figure includes some civilian camp followers and refugees from Moscow, but by no means all. Some 175,000 French army horses were also lost, along with nearly 1,500 guns. Between 1813 and peace in May 1814 the Russians released 100,000 prisoners of war, a few thousand staying on in Russia having been offered citizenship, a place in the ranks of the Russo-German Legion or, like Dr Roos or the Frenchman who became lecturer in French Literature at Kharkhov University, regular, peaceful employment.

Russian losses had been tremendous too. Some 250,000 regular troops had perished or gone missing, and tens of thousands were crippled or maimed. Losses amongst the Russian population have never been calculated but were certainly significant. Every town and most villages along the French line of march were in ruins. As winter turned to spring, epidemics began to break out along the route the French army had retreated and the campaign claimed countless more victims.

The Russian army, now much reduced and fatigued, arrived on the Niemen in January 1813. Despite Kutuzov's reluctance, the Russians crossed the river and took the war into Poland and Prussia. Sweden came out in open support of Russia on 7 January and, on 27 February 1813, Prussia too declared war on France. This was the decisive moment for the history of Napoleonic Europe. Napoleon's empire had frequently been bruised by the Peninsular War, but now imperial domination was shaken to its very core. Napoleon, with organisational genius, raised another army; but it could not match the Grande Armée of June 1812 in spirit or stamina. The Allies seized the initiative in the spring of 1813 and prepared themselves for the long, long march to Paris.

PREFACE TO THE FIRST EDITION

The authors of this work took part in the Russian campaign of 1812 as artillery officers in the 25th (Württemberg) Division of III Corps. They were eyewitnesses to the capricious fortunes of this war, sketches were made on the spot, and in 1827 the laborious task of drawing them up was begun – a task only completed in 1830.

The illustrations accurately portray the various scenes and situations in which the Grande Armée found itself. They cover the entire campaign from the beginning right through to the sinister climax as an army, accustomed to twenty years of victory and brilliant feats of arms, succumbs and is vanquished by northern frosts and by a struggle against insurmountable difficulties and constant want. It was this theme that motivated the author to have this work published.

The 25th Division formed part of III Corps, commanded by the brave Marshal Ney. It served, therefore, in the centre of the Grande Armée, under the orders of Napoleon, and played a key and glorious role in all the events of this war. Its actions helped Ney win the title Prince de Moskowa, after the battle of Borodino, and earned its general of division the honour of being promoted 'Count of the Empire'. The division's role, and the experiences of the men who fought in it, form a complete picture of events and fortunes unsurpassed in any other episode of military history.

Those who took part in the campaign will find in these pages a reminder of both the glorious and the terrible days of 1812; those who only know of the campaign from what they have read will now find all their reading brought to life. To some, this book will call to mind the events of the campaign and glorious feats of arms; to others it will reveal the terrible consequences of a disaster – one that, perhaps, they had the good fortune to escape.

This book places before you something which no one could describe in words alone; looking through it, you will accompany the Grande Armée to the Niemen; you will see our marches and camps; you will pass through such towns as Polotsk, Vitebsk, Smolensk, Viasma and Gjatsk; you will find yourself on the battlefields of Ostrovno, Krasnoi, Smolensk, Valutina-Gora and Borodino; you will gaze at the gilded domes and roofs of Moscow and watch the fire take hold; you will abandon Moscow with the army and head in the direction of Kaluga; then you will turn back to the old Moscow–Smolensk road and, witness to endless sacrifice, you will cross the snowy plains of Russia, pass through Krasnoi and Smolensk and arrive at the Beresina; you will cross the river and, passing through Vilna and Ponari, will finally regain the banks of the Niemen at Kovno.

The authors of this work served in Russia as artillery officers and were eyewitnesses to the events recorded here.

Major Faber du Faur
Major Kausler
1831

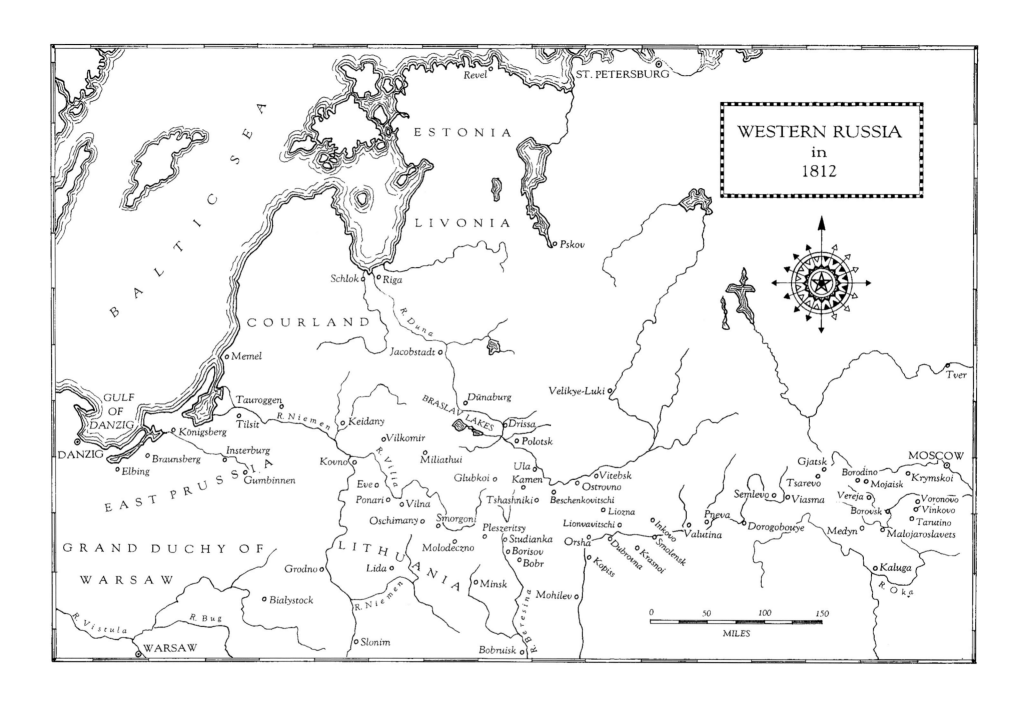

WESTERN RUSSIA
in
1812

BALTIC SEA

ESTONIA

Revel

ST. PETERSBURG

LIVONIA

Pskov

COURLAND

R. Duna

Schlok — *Riga*

Jacobstadt

Velikye-Luki

Tver

Memel

GULF
OF
DANZIG

Tauroggen

R. Niemen

Keidany

BRASLAV LAKES

Dünaburg

Drissa

Polotsk

Tilsit

Vilkomir

DANZIG

Königsberg

Kovno

R. Vilia

Miliathui

Ula

Vitebsk

Gjatsk

MOSCOW

Braunsberg

Insterburg

Kamen

Ostrovno

Tsarevo

Borodino

Krymskoi

Elbing

EAST PRUSSIA

Gumbinnen

Eve

Ponari

Vilna

Glubkoi

Tshashniki

Beschenkovitschi

Liozna

Semlevo

Viasma

Mojaisk

Voronovo

Vereja

Vinkovo

Borovsk

Tarutino

Oschimany

Smorgoni

Pleszeritsy

Lionvavitschi

Pneva

Valutina

Dorogobouye

Medyn

Malojaroslavets

GRAND DUCHY OF

LITHUANIA

Molodeczno

Studianka

Borisov

Orsha

Dubrovna

Krasnoi

Inkovo

Smolensk

WARSAW

Grodno

Lida

Bobr

Kopiss

Kaluga

R. Oka

Bialystock

R. Niemen

Minsk

R. Beresina

Mohilev

R. Vistula

R. Bug

Slonim

Bobruisk

WARSAW

0   50   100   150

MILES

18

THE PLATES

1
ON THE BANKS OF THE NIEMEN, 25 JUNE

In the second half of June, all the troops destined to take part in the war against Russia were assembling between the Vistula and the Niemen and were marching towards the enemy frontier.

An auxiliary corps of 30,000 Austrians, under the orders of Prince Schwarzenberg, on the way from Galicia, formed the right wing; X Corps, also of 30,000 men, and commanded by Marshal Macdonald, Duke of Tarentum, formed the left.

The Grande Armée was concentrated between these two wings in three distinct bodies. The first, under the King of Westphalia, was composed of V, VII and VIII Corps – some 70,000 Poles, Saxons and Westphalians under Poniatowski, Reynier and King Jerome – and supported the Austrians by marching on Grodno. The second, to the left of these troops, was under Prince Eugène, Viceroy of Italy, and was composed of 50,000 Italians and Bavarians of IV and VI Corps (the latter commanded by St Cyr). The last, and strongest, force was to fight under Napoleon himself and comprised at least 200,000 men: Guards, under the Dukes of Istria and Danzig; cavalry under Murat, king of Naples; and I, II and III Corps (the latter including the 25th Württemberg Division) commanded by Davout, Prince of Eckmühl, and the Dukes of Reggio (Oudinot) and d'Elchingen (Ney). This force was to cross the Niemen near Kovno.

On 23 June the first elements of the imperial column reached the banks of the Niemen just to the south of Kovno, near Poniemen. During the night of the 23rd/24th three pontoon bridges were thrown across the river and, on the 24th, at dawn, the army began to set foot on enemy territory. III Corps, which had broken camp at Kalvary on the 24th, advanced towards Ludovinovo and Marienpol by forced marches, and arrived at Poniemen that evening. Our march had been arduous, and had in part been through a burning forest, but the corps camped alongside other troops and looked down over a majestic scene. The night was brilliant, illuminated by countless campfires scattered along the valley and on the slopes of the heights. Even more impressive was the scene the next day as the troops formed up between the dying campfires and, dazzling in the gleaming rays of sunshine, marched for the bridges. Morale was high, there was courage aplenty, and all were animated by boundless optimism. Each soldier strove to reach Russian soil, and it seemed the finest and most warlike army ever assembled. Who could have thought that, of all these thousands of men sent to do battle in Russia, so few would re-cross, in total disorder, the icy Niemen in just five months' time?

2
CAMP OF HIS HIGHNESS, THE PRINCE ROYAL OF WÜRTTEMBERG, NEAR EVE, 28 JUNE

The forced marches we had made before the Niemen, combined with those that had taken place after crossing the river, and which had taken us towards Vilna, had made a day of rest essential for III Corps. The Corps, after a fourteen-hour march, arrived at Eve on the night of the 27th. It was exhausted, hungry and considerably weakened by a haemorrhage of stragglers. Therefore, the 28th was set aside for the recuperation of the Württemberg division.

We camped on to the fringe of a lush forest and, before long, huts made of leaves and branches were thrown up to provide sweet-smelling shelter and form a temporary town. The first such hut was made for our very own prince, the hope of our nation. He had borne the want, the fatigues and the dangers equally with his comrades and was now to rest beneath branches just like the most lowly of his soldiers.

This rest-day allowed us to recover our strength somewhat, and, on the 29th, we set out for the Vilia in order to try and attempt a crossing of that river.

3
NEAR EVE, 29 JUNE

There has never been a campaign in which the troops have relied so much on living off the land, but it was the way it was done in Russia that caused such universal suffering – for the soldiers of the army as well as for the inhabitants. Because of its rapid marches and its enormous size, the army faced a dearth of everything and it was impossible to procure even the barest necessity.

It was around the time that we reached Eve that one can date the start of this fatal requisitioning and the destruction of the surrounding countryside, which, naturally, had devastating consequences. Every day, as we broke camp, we could see clouds of marauders and isolated bodies of troops make off in all directions, setting off to find the barest of essentials. They would return to camp in the evening, laden with their booty.

Inevitably, this kind of behaviour made an unfortunate impression on Lithuania, which had so long been under the yoke of Russia and, instead of any benefit from its new alliance, saw only the pillaging and oppression wrought by its new allies. In addition, discipline was sapped, and tolerating or turning a blind eye to these misdemeanours, whether or not they really benefited the troops, only speeded up the destruction of this potentially formidable army.

4
BETWEEN KIRGALICZKY AND SUDERVA, 30 JUNE

On 29 June III Corps left Eve and, around noon, marched into Kirgaliczky on the Vilia – a river considerably swollen by incessant rain. The bridge had been burnt and we halted on the banks of the river whilst a pontoon bridge was thrown across. On the 30th, early in the afternoon, the bridge was deemed ready and III Corps filed across to the far bank. The rain continued to fall in torrents and, as well as turning our camp into a bog, had soaked the ground, making it almost impossible to march.

On the far bank we had to climb some rather steep heights in order to get to Suderva, and it was extremely difficult getting the limbers forward. After a few guns and caissons had struggled to the crest of the heights – but then only by using double teams of horses – those that followed found the ground so churned up that guns and limbers sank up to their axles. It was therefore necessary to find an alternative route but, for the reasons already mentioned, this new route was similarly rendered impassable. Hundreds of horses expired and, half-submerged in the mire, marked the course of III Corps. This particular march cost us so many horses that we had to leave a battery of 12-pounder guns, and the bulk of our reserve, at Vilna for want of draught animals to pull them.

5
CAMP AT MILIATHUI, 5 JULY

III Corps advanced as far as Miliathui by forced marches but, upon reaching that place, was allowed to rest so that the stragglers might catch up. We were only two weeks into the campaign, but already the scarcity of food was such that a single loaf of bread cost six crowns. The troops therefore found it essential to lay their hands on silver in order to obtain the barest necessities. Even animal skins became an object of trade and were sold to local Jews. This trade was, nevertheless, of considerable use to the army.

Faber du Faur del.

gedr. v. C. Küstner

6
NEAR TSCHOULANOUI, 7 JULY

On 6 July the 25th Division took up position close to Tschoulanoui, in the midst of a pleasant, fertile countryside littered with fields of corn and beautiful forests. But this region was soon to suffer the full horrors of war. We were not issued with any food, nor did we come across supplies or inhabitants willing to sell them; we were, as before, obliged to scour the land with detachments and take what we needed by force. We left Tschoulanoui on the 9th, leaving no trace of having been there but empty barns, despoiled fields and thinned-out forests.

v. Faber du Faur del.   O. Kästner gedruckt.   F. Bruninger lith.

7
CAMP AT KOKUTICZKI, 9 JULY

In a land where we were entirely ignorant of the language, the large number of Jews in the area proved to be a great advantage. Whilst everyone else had fled at first sight of the soldiers, and were hiding in the forests, these people did not leave their huts. Long since accustomed to mistreatment and suspicion, they still looked upon our presence as a new opportunity for trade. As they spoke our language perfectly, they served as excellent guides right from the initial crossing of the Russian frontier. Even so, we frequently had to employ a measure of force to ensure that they carried out this occasionally dangerous task, and any obstinacy on the part of the Jews was met by a quick beating from the soldiers.

8
NEAR KOZUSCZINA, 11 JULY

The army had crossed the Niemen carrying supplies for eight days, as the intention had been to get to Vilna and gain a decisive victory. The transports carrying the supplies would follow on behind the army and a decisive battle would do the rest, but, as the Russians continued to retreat, so the chances of the crucial battle diminished. Had we halted, so we would have given up any chance of preventing Bagration's and Barclay-de-Tolly's armies from linking up and of being able to defeat them in detail. So we pursued the enemy closely and 400,000 men found themselves fighting day after day without supplies, in a land devastated by friend and foe and which had, with some difficulty, only just sustained the handful of Swedes led by Charles XII.

The main body under Napoleon, of which III Corps was a part, suffered badly. It marched along the main road, already stripped bare by the French vanguard, which had consumed everything not already burnt by the Russians in their retreat. The corps was reduced to the necessity of sending out large bodies of men every morning to scour the neighbouring villages some way off the main road. These mobile detachments had orders to carry off all foodstuffs and, after sweeping the flanks of the corps, were to return to the ranks in the evening. Most of these detachments obtained small Russian horses to make their task easier, and these animals served as beasts of burden if wagons could not be obtained. Every evening we witnessed the return of these cavalrymen to camp and saw that, instead of leading their mounts, they rode into camp perched on top of their loot.

v. Faber du Faur del. Bartmeister lith.

9
CAMP AT RASKIMOSI, BY THE BRASLAV LAKE, 18 JULY

On 15 July we broke camp at Drisviatoni and, arriving on the shores of Lake Braslav, we settled down for the night at Raskimosi. We stayed there until the 19th, making desperate attempts to rid ourselves of dysentery which, because of our exertions, our lack of supplies and the poor climate, had wrought havoc in our ranks. This disease took hold so suddenly, and with such mortal consequences, that, during the march or in the camp itself, it was not unusual to see men suddenly collapse without having shown any symptoms whatsoever. The staff were not spared either, and numbers were carried off by this plague. Even the Crown Prince, glorious commander, did not go untouched, and he was taken to Vilna to recover, where he lay on a sickbed for a number of days.

Later, we learned that Barclay had abandoned the entrenched camp at Drissa and that he had made off for Vitebsk. This led to our quitting our camp at Raskimosi, on the 19th, and, as with all the troops under the direct command of Napoleon, attempting to beat Barclay to Vitebsk or, at the very least, forcing him to offer battle.

The roads had been rendered almost impassable by endless convoys, although logs had been laid over the mud at particularly marshy points. These problems led to endless bickering between various bodies of troops, who would all try to push past each other in order to get forwards; nobody intervened to end the disorder, and this particular march was the most difficult we had had to undertake in this campaign. Only on the 21st did we halt, utterly exhausted, and camp by a road and close by a burning village.

On 22 July III Corps set about establishing camp at Disna, not far from the Duna; the corps then departed on the morning of the 23rd for Polotsk, leaving behind a brigade of infantry and a battery of our artillery. These troops were to await the arrival of II Corps.

No sooner had the bulk of the corps marched off than the inhabitants of the surrounding countryside reappeared and scoured the camp for anything our troops might have left behind. For the most part they were reclaiming materials taken from the surrounding villages, such as wood, utensils and so on.

Finally, towards evening, we saw the columns of II Corps appear and we set out for Polotsk and for a reunion with our own corps.

10
BEFORE POLOTSK, 25 JULY

It was in the evening of the 24th, after a most arduous march through a swampy forest, that we arrived at Polotsk, a town of 4,000 inhabitants in Vitebsk province, some 685 versts from Moscow and at the confluence of the Polota and Duna rivers. We camped outside the town, and the following morning we continued our march, heading for Beschenkovitschi, just as the first rays of sunshine played brilliantly on the town's church towers and steeples. Of all the churches, the Jesuit College was the most impressive. The Jesuit Order, which had been excluded from all countries except Russia, had its principal base here, along with its own printing press. The Order's general lived here; so too did 44 priests, 46 students and 29 novices.

Polotsk was destined for military fame as there would be battles fought here on 17 and 18 August as well as on 18 and 19 October.

11
ON THE RIGHT BANK OF THE DUNA, BELOW POLOTSK, 25 JULY

From Polotsk the road follows the right bank of the Duna for some way until, after an hour's march, you come across a wonderful château surrounded by gardens and substantial buildings. This was probably the great house at Strudnia, a place often mentioned in Bavarian accounts because of the inhabitants' heroic defence of the bridge which here straddles the river. The place was deserted by its owners, had been pillaged and was full of stragglers of all nations doing whatever they wanted. This march, and indeed all the marches we made in our attempts to catch up with III Corps, from which we had been separated in the defiles of Polotsk forest, followed in the wake of the main body of the Grande Armée. This made us witnesses to the sheer horror and hideous aspect of this way of waging war. The dead and the dying, victims of all the forced marches, general want and rigours of the climate, lay strewn across the road and on either side of it. The villages, great houses and byways were full of stragglers, some of whom were preoccupied in trying to get back to their units; others, on the other hand, deliberately hung about waiting for the army to pass them by so that they could then make off.

Long columns of livestock and little Russian wagons filled with supplies followed the columns, and the whole resembled more the exodus of an entire people than the finest army of Europe commanded by the greatest captain of the age.

v. Faber du Faur del.   C. Küstner gedr.   Baumeister, Federer lith.

12
CAMP AT ULA, 26 JULY

After overcoming the hardships, and various dangers, we succeeded in reaching our objective of Ula – a small town by a stream of the same name, mostly inhabited by Jews – after marching close by burning fields and meadows. We were almost consumed by a further fire when the little town itself went up in flames – no doubt set on fire by the carelessness of the bands of malingerers of all nations and all arms – but fortunately we had resolved to march through Ula and established our camp on the far side of the town. The fire made such progress that a good number of buildings were soon reduced to cinders.

13
NEAR BESCHENKOVITSCHI, 28 JULY, AT 5.00 IN THE MORNING

The Viceroy of Italy had clashed with the Russian rearguard of Barclay's army, commanded by Dokhturov, close by Beschenkovitschi. He had pushed the Russians back and repaired the bridge burnt down by the Russians as they retreated.

Beschenkovitschi is a pretty little town built largely on the right bank of the Duna in a most picturesque landscape. The town had a number of beautiful churches and a large synagogue; it was 635 versts from Moscow and 59 versts from Vitebsk. We arrived late on the 27th but were disappointed to find that our division had moved out earlier that day. We came across just three battalions; these had been ordered to defend the bridge over the Duna and we had been detailed to join them in this duty. We established ourselves just outside Beschenkovitschi, along the road to Ostrovno and not far from an imposing church. On the 28th we took up the positions assigned to us for the defence of the bridge. Our battery was placed on the left bank of the Duna, half of it in the town, half to the right of the bridge itself.

14
NEAR BESCHENKOVITSCHI, ON THE BANKS OF THE DUNA, 29 JULY

Napoleon was pursuing the enemy in an attempt to run him to ground and force him to do battle. Meanwhile our troops had set alight one of Beschenkovitschi's suburbs in order to construct earthworks so that, in case of some kind of reverse, our retreat would be assured. A cloud of black smoke toiled above the town and soon the Russian houses, mostly built of wood, were consigned to the flames and burnt to cinders. To cover the bridge we had placed one of our guns on the road to Krukovieczi, at a bend in the river.

15
SUBURBS OF BESCHENKOVITSCHI, ON THE RIGHT BANK OF THE DUNA, 29 JULY

To defend the bridge it had been deemed necessary to throw up some defensive earthworks. This entailed the destruction of one of the town's suburbs. One of the buildings destroyed in the ensuing conflagration was a beautiful wooden church. Here I depict that church for posterity so that it might not be entirely forgotten.

16
BESCHENKOVITSCHI, 30 JULY

However much we had need of some rest after our arduous marches, which had exhausted both man and horse, we were nonetheless somewhat unsettled by the idea that the army had moved on to new exploits whilst we were left here guarding a bridge. We, man and horse alike, slept in barns and sheds, leaving our cannon out in the open. Our men, happy to have some shelter and free from sad presentiments of a horrible future, indulged in some sweet idleness and spent their time dreaming of the land they had left behind them or telling stories. On the 30th our rest came to an end as we were relieved by Bavarians and received the order to march towards Vitebsk, by forced marches, to re-join the army.

14
NEAR BESCHENKOVITSCHI, ON THE BANKS OF THE DUNA, 29 JULY

Napoleon was pursuing the enemy in an attempt to run him to ground and force him to do battle. Meanwhile our troops had set alight one of Beschenkovitschi's suburbs in order to construct earthworks so that, in case of some kind of reverse, our retreat would be assured. A cloud of black smoke toiled above the town and soon the Russian houses, mostly built of wood, were consigned to the flames and burnt to cinders. To cover the bridge we had placed one of our guns on the road to Krukovieczi, at a bend in the river.

v Peter die Paur del.   C Küstner gude   Baumeister Federer lith.

12
CAMP AT ULA, 26 JULY

After overcoming the hardships, and various dangers, we succeeded in reaching our objective of Ula – a small town by a stream of the same name, mostly inhabited by Jews – after marching close by burning fields and meadows. We were almost consumed by a further fire when the little town itself went up in flames – no doubt set on fire by the carelessness of the bands of malingerers of all nations and all arms – but fortunately we had resolved to march through Ula and established our camp on the far side of the town. The fire made such progress that a good number of buildings were soon reduced to cinders.

17
ON THE ROAD BETWEEN BESCHENKOVITSCHI AND OSTROVNO, 31 JULY

On the 31st we were relieved by the Bavarians and departed from Beschenkovitschi in order to re-join our division at Liozna.

The two days of march that we made in order to re-join our corps presented an unforgettable glimpse of the shocking state of the army. The same dismal scene presented itself upon each successive day – exhausted soldiers oblivious to exhortations, threats or punishment. At each halt, each camp, we noticed that the number of effective troops had diminished. We hoped that at the first opportunity, at the first rest day, the stragglers would catch up and re-join the ranks. Vain hope! The vast majority of these exhausted soldiers soon turned into corpses marking the twisted route of the army.

We were only two leagues from Beschenkovitschi when we came across some more corpses. Two of them belonged to our light infantry; one of them even had his tunic on back to front – the punishment meted out to those who had been caught straggling in the rear. We took the opportunity of a brief halt to bury these unfortunates.

18
NEAR OSTROVNO, 1 AUGUST

During the course of our march to Liozna we marched through both Ostrovno and Vitebsk. The first of these two places had been the scene, on 25 July, of a clash between Murat and Ostermann. We saw the traces of the engagement for the next three days as we marched along the main road. The road was littered with the debris of arms and equipment, and even corpses, right up to the walls of Vitebsk. Dead men and dead horses showed the various positions of the Russians and that the attacks of Murat and Eugène had taken place on a narrow front – no doubt caused by the thick forests which ran along the edge of the road for most of the way. The bodies had been exposed to the burning heat of the summer sun and they were rotting. It was a horrible sight and the air was thick for some distance with the stench of death. Our march through this scene was next to impossible.

19
IN THE LIOZNA CAMP, 4 AUGUST

The army had much need of a rest and the Emperor ordered it to halt and make camp. V Corps camped at Mohilev, I Corps at Orscha, Dubrovna and Luibovitscji; Murat's cavalry, IV Corps and the Imperial Guard extended from Orscha and Dubrovna to Vitebsk and Suray; III Corps, and our division, were encamped at Liozna. Our outposts stretched as far as Lyadi, Inkovo and Veli.

We were glad of the rest, but our greatest fear during the march had been how to feed ourselves and this fear followed us into our cantonments. We were obliged to send out detachments to find and bring in our daily alimentary needs. But the scarcity of supplies soon began to make itself felt – the region had to support a vast number of troops and was soon exhausted. Behind us, the way we had come, everything had been consumed or destroyed; we were flanked by troops from different corps in exactly the same situation as ourselves; in front of us was our vanguard and the entire Russian army under the orders of Barclay and Bagration. Our days of rest were not as we had imagined them. This sudden activity, after so many forced marches, the scarce and unwholesome food, the roasting summer days followed by bitterly cold nights – all this sowed sickness and death among our ranks. No sooner had we sent one batch of sick off to the hospitals of Vitebsk than the houses of Liozna were again filled with our sick, whilst the gardens and ditches were full of our dead.

Our losses became most apparent when we were reviewed by Marshal Ney on 5 August. Our infantry, which had not fired a shot, had lost half its effective strength; our artillery had had to make use of some infantry to replace its losses and we had replaced the 152 horses we had lost with 280 Russian horses.

20
NEAR LIOZNA, 6 AUGUST

Our prolonged stay between the Duna and the Dnepr allowed the swarms of stragglers, from all arms, to re-join their various units. If poor food and inclement weather had thinned the ranks of the army, then green forage had done the same for the army's horses – thousands, particularly French and German, had died. The cavalry, deprived of many of their mounts, sought out native Russian horses, something easily done as they ran practically wild in the woods.

It was both sad and amusing to see these stubborn and emaciated beasts trot past our camp, ridden by massive carabiniers and cuirassiers with their shiny boots virtually touching the ground.

21
IN THE LIOZNA CAMP, 6 AUGUST

Our stay at Liozna at least allowed us to lay our hands on some of the comforts of life – something that had been impossible during our all too rapid advance when we hardly ever camped in the same place two nights in a row. We built ourselves a proper camp at Liozna. From materials furnished by the very fields, i.e. the yellowing corn, we constructed artful shelters. The regiments of III Corps competed to see which unit would have the most elegant shelters. Ours, placed close by a newly planted forest, on a patch of ground formerly used for the training of draught horses, had every convenience that could be expected under the circumstances.

However, our stay at Liozna presented us with ample opportunity to ponder the serious position we found ourselves in and whatever the future might hold. Despite the privations felt in the army, the serene sky, the rolling countryside and a whole host of pleasant scenes still managed to make an impression. Routine chores helped lighten our mood and the cares weighing down upon us. Here you could come across soldiers cooking or washing; further on you might find troops herding the livestock that we had dragged with us. Such events took place every day and every hour, with endless variations.

a. Faber du Faur pri. C. Küstner gedr. F. Valroix lith.

22
IN THE LIOZNA CAMP, 11 AUGUST

The officers' shelters were built with care and attention to every detail, and were superior to those of the soldiers. That of the officers of the 2nd battery, as depicted here, was set in a pretty little glade, amongst beech and hazel trees, with the soldiers' huts placed all around it. The shelter had been built with considerable skill by some artillerymen – builders by profession – using sheaves of corn. All the tables and chairs, even the door (an oil painting of Christ on the cross), had been taken from a pillaged château. It was all very comfortable.

v. Faber du Faur gem.   G. Küstner gedr.   Domingos d. Raumsater lith.

23
IN THE VICINITY OF LIONVAVITSCHI, 13 AUGUST

The Emperor, who must have calculated that the entire Russian army was before us, abandoned the line of operations of Vitebsk, preferring that of Minsk. He therefore pushed 180,000 men against the enemy's left flank and rear in order to cut him off, if possible, from Smolensk, Moscow and southern Russia. Operations began on the 12th. The Guard, Murat's cavalry, three divisions of I Corps, III Corps and IV Corps all marched off to the right in order to cross the Dnepr.

We broke camp on the 12th and, after a two-day march of considerable difficulty, we drew close to the banks of that river.

a Faber du Faur gem.

G. Küstner gedr.

Emminger u. Baumeister lith.

24
CROSSING OF THE BORYSTHENE, 14 AUGUST

On the morning of 14 August, after a short march, we reached the right bank of the Borysthene, just opposite Khomino. Preparations had been made for our crossing. Three ramps ran down the sloping banks of the river to the water's edge – two were for the cavalry and artillery, one was for the infantry. The infantry were to use a bridge, the others were supposed to ford across. A huge artillery park and convoys of wagons were massed on the right bank, awaiting their chance to cross. The crush was horrific as troops, guns and wagons all sought to get to the ramps and get over first. There was considerable disorder and no one saw fit to try and impose some discipline on the multitude. The disorder was made worse by the sound of firing in the distance – everyone strove harder to gain the far bank in order to get to grips with the enemy at long last. The firing was caused by a running battle between Murat's cavalry and some Cossacks. The latter were attempting to cut some bridges on the Krasnoi road.

25
KRASNOI, 14 AUGUST

In the afternoon of the 14th Ney and Murat arrived before Krasnoi, a small village some twenty miles from Smolensk. A Russian infantry regiment had barricaded itself in the village but was forced out by Ledru's division. It fell back and joined some five or six thousand Russians positioned on the Smolensk road and supported by artillery and cavalry. It was Neverovskii's division. These troops had been surprised and now found themselves on a plain stretching for miles, amongst the ripening cornfields. The Russians were now entirely exposed to the charges of our cavalry. Only a small stream separated the two opposing sides, and problems encountered by our cavalry as it tried to cross this stream gave Neverovskii time to ready himself and form his infantry up into one huge square. No sooner had he done this than he saw his cavalry charged and flee in disorder and his artillery taken, whilst his infantry were forced to withstand the massed attack of the cavalry. He set his square in motion despite being assailed by Murat's cavalry – he would owe his survival as much to the tenacity of his own troops as to Murat's poorly directed attacks and impatience. As soon as the guns of our 2nd horse artillery battery opened up with a devastating discharge of canister, Murat, brandishing his sabre, charged across our muzzles and we would have to cease fire as the massed cavalry prevented our firing again. The Russians would then re-form, their ranks leaving no trace of any loss, and would continue their retreat.

And so it went on from position to position. The Russians eventually reached a wooded defile and, with their flanks covered, they managed to slip away towards the safety of Smolensk having lost 2,000 men.

26
SMOLENSK, 16 AUGUST

Neverovskii reached Smolensk with his division and warned of our imminent arrival. The city is at the foot of the range of hills that form a narrow valley for the Borysthene. This river divides the city into two parts and these are connected by two bridges and a number of fords. That which is usually termed the old town sits on the slopes of the left bank and is fortified in true Tartar style – the defences are attributed to Boris Gudonov. The wall that surrounds this part of the city is 3,000 toises long, 25 feet high and 18 feet thick. It is topped with whitewashed battlements and replete with twenty-nine towers. In addition to the outer defences there is a citadel – a system of earthworks – and some of the suburbs have their own defences. That part of the city on the right bank of the river has a number of beautiful buildings. It is a more modern development but can no longer be considered as just a suburb; it stretches from the river to the base of the surrounding hills and is, with the exception of a *tête de pont*, completely undefended.

The army, following in Neverovskii's bloody footsteps, arrived before the city at noon on the 16th. Murat and Poniatowski were sent against the right, where the river enters the city, and formed our right flank. Davout, with I Corps, took up positions in the centre, whilst Ney, with III Corps, formed the left flank. Ney's corps had Razout's division on the right, Ledru in the centre and the 25th Division (Württembergers) on the left. Our division pushed down towards the Borysthene, as it exits from the city, and thus completed the investment of the place.

The Russians were pushed back to the walls themselves. As they retreated we sent the König Regiment of Jägers after them, but these sustained heavy casualties. The Old and Young Guard were kept in reserve, along with Eugène's Italians.

All we could see from where we were positioned were the cupolas of the cathedral, a part of the Borysthene and the range of hills on the other side of the river, our view being obscured by the wooded hills around us. We could see in the distance long, trailing columns kicking up swirling clouds of dust as they marched towards Smolensk. Some thought that this must be Junot, who was supposed to be carrying out a flanking movement, and they hoped to see him attack the Russians at any moment. Soon, however, the columns reached the Russian positions. It was the entire Russian army under Barclay and Bagration. Brought to their senses by the attack on Neverovskii, the Russians were now rushing to the aid of the city and so as not to be cut off from the road to Moscow.

27
SMOLENSK, 17 AUGUST, AT 10.00 IN THE EVENING

At dawn on the 17th firing commenced all along the line, and this continued, with just a few brief pauses, until noon. In the afternoon the firing grew even more intense; the Emperor, having arrived on the scene, was sure that the Russians would not risk a battle out in the open but were opting to defend the city itself. He therefore gave the order to attack Smolensk at all points. The brave Poles of Poniatowski, supported by their sixty cannon, advanced on the right and attacked the suburbs, hoping to cut one of the bridges. Morand and Gudin, of Davout's corps, attacked some fortified suburbs in the centre of the position. Ney, at the head of his veteran columns, attacked along the Dnepr, engaging those Russians positioned outside the western rampart. The fighting was fierce and bloody, but our troops succeeded in pushing back the enemy. The Russians now withdrew behind the city walls, and we called off our attack. In vain did the artillery of III Corps and the Imperial Guard direct its fire against these walls, echoing the rumble of the Russian artillery positioned on the ramparts and towers. In vain did we try to silence their artillery by bombarding those very ramparts and towers. In vain did the Guard's 12-pounders and I Corps' artillery advance, coming under fire as they did so, in an attempt to effect a breach in those magnificent walls. All our attempts failed, and night put an end to this combat, which had had a cost out of all proportion to the results gained. It was then, however, that a new spectacle met our eyes. We could see the cupolas of the cathedral from our camp, and, as we looked down on the city, we caught sight of huge columns of flames roaring up from the heart of Smolensk. The flames became more intense, forming a ball of fire that turned night to day and lit the countryside for miles around. The fire, fanned by the gentle breezes of a summer evening, called to mind Vesuvius. We were as if enchanted, and thought neither of our current plight nor of the terrible consequences this fire would have for us.

28
SMOLENSK, 18 AUGUST, AT 6.00 IN THE MORNING

The Russians, cooped up inside Smolensk and threatened with being cut off, set fire to the buildings on the left bank, pulled back over the river and burnt the bridges behind them. But they did not as yet abandon the suburb situated on the right bank, which is almost as extensive as the town and dominates it thanks to the range of heights which sweeps down almost to the water's edge.

We occupied the smoking remains of the town at dawn on the 18th and our division then received the order to ford the river and attack the suburb.

Our first line infantry brigade quickly advanced, crossed the river, seized the *tête de pont* and chased the Russians through the streets. We then advanced against the heights, but, finding them defended by superior forces and numerous artillery, our troops were driven back and almost over the river, clinging only to the *tête de pont* and a few houses and gardens along the riverbank.

Our light brigade and the second of our line brigades were rushed forward in support. Our artillery, positioned close by a small chapel, was also ordered into the fray.

29
BY THE WALLS OF SMOLENSK, 18 AUGUST

We obeyed the order to move forward as quickly as our emaciated horses would allow us, rushing through the streets on the left bank and rolling over the piles of dead littering the ground. We were directed by Marshal Ney in person to take up a position on a hill, between two polygon towers, from which we could bombard the Russians. From there we could observe the entire right bank, and could enfilade the entire length of one of the principal streets. Thus it was, with the aid of a battery of light French pieces to our left, that we could continue the struggle. But it proved just as impossible to flush the Russians out of the houses and gardens as it did to harm those taking cover behind the weeping willows on the right bank. Their fire was inflicting casualties on us.

The enemy held out obstinately until the evening, when the excessive heat generated by the numerous fires drove friend and foe out of the suburb.

Some of our gunners, exhausted by their exertions, and tormented by a thirst inflicted by the heat of a scorching summer day, came across a Russian girl in one of the houses and made her fetch water for them. Intimidated by the sight of these strange warriors, and terrorised by the thunder of the guns and sinister whistling of shells, she visibly trembled as she drew close to the scene of the struggle. Even so, fortune was with her as, after carrying water to us a number of times at the risk of life and limb, she eventually managed to return safe and sound to the bosom of her worried family.

30
BY THE WALLS OF SMOLENSK, 18 AUGUST

No sooner had our valiant troops established themselves in the suburb on the right bank of the river than they were assailed from all sides by masses of enemy troops. We rushed a few pieces forward to support our men, but these soon came under Russian fire. Before long we found ourselves positioned on ground that, not long ago, had been occupied by the enemy's battalions. The ground was littered with the debris of their equipment, and this served to remind us of the ferocity of the struggle. Cannon balls still bounced towards us, ploughing through the soil and showering us with earth and stones. Even if the missiles went harmlessly by, and we thought the danger over, a number of us were still wounded by cannon balls ricocheting off the walls behind us and once again falling into our ranks.

Faber du Faur del.

31
BY THE WALLS OF SMOLENSK, 18 AUGUST, AT 5.00 IN THE EVENING

Evening restored a little calm. The day was coming to an end and, apart from having to fire an occasional shot, we found ourselves rendered mere spectators to the scene which was literally being played out under our feet. There was continual skirmishing, but it seemed as though the fighting was dying down, particularly as the various fires, which had broken out here and there, had made such progress as to render movement in the streets virtually impossible. We could not tell whether or not the fire had been started by the Russians themselves, to impede our progress or destroy provisions hoarded in the town, or had been caused by the fighting. Or perhaps it was a combination of these two factors? Whatever the cause, it remains a mystery to this day.

Meanwhile, as these scenes were being played out on the right bank, the masses of the Grande Armée were gathering on the left bank, forming up on the heights above the town. To the strains of martial music they began filing down towards the Borysthene, in preparation for the crossing of that river the very next day.

It was an imposing scene complete with impressive music: the firing of Russian artillery, which, positioned on the heights opposite, sought to bring fire to bear on our massed ranks; the groan of our own artillery firing in reply and attempting to silence the Russian guns. All this, on a beautiful summer's evening, in the delightful, rolling countryside around Smolensk, branded our souls with a magic that is impossible to describe and that will live forever in the minds of all who were present at the scene.

32
BY THE WALLS OF SMOLENSK, 18 AUGUST, AT 10.00 IN THE EVENING

The rumble of cannon fire gradually died away and firing had virtually ceased. The conflagration had come between the two opposing armies and had made itself the master of the battlefield. A cannon fired the final shot of 18 August and the fighting was over. A profound silence descended – a silence broken by the roar of flames devouring houses. Our troops had gathered and were resting after the day's ordeals. Even so, our hearts cried out for a good number of troops who had quitted the campfires that morning never to return. Many fell by the river, having fallen in the assault of the bridgehead or in the street fighting. Those that died quickly probably died well. If, wounded, they lay in the streets at the mercy of a roaring inferno, they would surely be consumed by that merciless fire.

At 10 o'clock we were gathered in that part of the town untouched by the fire, the reflection of which was dancing on the surface of the river and off the surface of the Tartar walls and towers. The whole area was lit up, but the scene was of but short duration. Even before midnight the fire abated and the most beautiful, the richest part of Smolensk, which had been such an imposing sight that morning, now lay as smouldering, flaming cinders amongst smoking rubble.

33
SMOLENSK, ON THE RIGHT BANK OF THE BORYSTHENE, 19 AUGUST

On the 18th our efforts to flush the Russians out from the gardens and from behind the willows on the banks of the Dnepr had been unsuccessful. They maintained a well-nourished fire throughout the day, targeting our infantry in the houses on the left bank and causing casualties among our artillery positioned below the walls of the town. Amongst the enemy sharpshooters there was one in particular who distinguished himself by his bravery and perseverance. We singled him out, training a French gun, positioned to our left, against him and attempting, literally, to smash the willow trees and deprive him of his cover. But we could not silence the man. It was only when it grew dark that his firing ceased; we thought at first that he must have been pulled back as the Russians retreated but, as we later found, that was not the reason. On the 19th, as we secured the right bank and made our way to the position occupied by the Russian light infantrymen, we discovered the lone Russian sharpshooter just by the afore-mentioned willows. He was a non-commissioned officer in a Chasseur regiment and his body was partially covered by the debris of the broken willows. He had not abandoned his post, which he had so gloriously defended the day before, but had been killed by a round shot.

34
ON THE STABNA, 19 AUGUST

What horrors met our eyes as we passed through the ruins of the St Petersburg suburb, where the fire had run its awful course! We marched through rubble and piles of ashes, over smoking ruins and hundreds of shrivelled corpses. We despaired at the sight of shakos and helmets, which the flames had not been able to consume, and at the charred corpses – all that remained of our brothers-in-arms and countrymen who thus had died, consumed by the fire after having fallen, grievously wounded, in the street fighting the day before.

Our advance was cautious in the extreme, believing as we did that the Russian rearguard might ambush us and fall upon us at any moment. We eventually reached the junction of the Moscow and St Petersburg roads and, after pushing out reconnaissance parties, discovered that the Russians had taken the road to Moscow, which follows the Dnepr, and were but little distance from Smolensk. They were drawn up on the heights on the opposite banks of the Stabna, a small tributary of the Dnepr, after having destroyed the bridges over this river, and they also occupied the village of the same name. They welcomed us by showering our left flank with a devastating discharge of shot and shell.

Marshal Ney, who was present on the field of battle, ordered Ledru's and Razout's divisions to advance down the Moscow road in columns of companies. The 25th was directed to form up in line to cover their left flank and III Corps' artillery to counter the fire of the Russian batteries. The advance began. The Russians were pushed back from their initial position after about an hour of fighting; they took up a second position behind Valutina-Gora and prepared to receive us in a far more determined manner.

35
BETWEEN SMOLENSK AND VALUTINA-GORA, 19 AUGUST

After that initial encounter we repaired the bridges over the Stabna and pushed forward as fast as we could, III Corps leading the way. We advanced along the Moscow road, but also attempted to make our way over the wooded heights on the left, aiming to cut off the Russians as they fell back in retreat. Even our artillery was told to follow this route – an order which could only be executed with much loss and suffering. But we were considerably distracted by magnificent views over the Dnepr valley and I spent the time it took us to gain the summit of those troublesome heights sketching the scene you see opposite.

In the foreground can be seen the foot of the heights we are about to ascend; in the background we catch sight of the Dnepr valley; picturesque hills cradle the river on either side; whilst, at our feet, are the long columns of troops snaking their way out of Smolensk. We can see Smolensk's superb cathedral and the city's white walls, partially obscured by the black smoke which still pours forth from the city and from the suburb on the right bank. The suburb, which, by now, was nothing more than a pile of rubble, was masked by the heights that reached down to the riverbank. Nevertheless, the convent on the heights above can be seen. This convent marked one of the principal positions of the Russians on the 17th and 18th. There they established two twenty-gun batteries, and these rained down a veritable shower of missiles on to our artillery and sought to make any crossing of the river, or any attempt to establish ourselves on the right bank, impossible.

36
NEAR VALUTINA-GORA, 19 AUGUST

Our corps, with the 11th Division to the fore, followed the Russian rearguard for a number of hours until it took up a position near Valutina-Gora and made ready to accept battle.

Barclay had not followed the Moscow road but had instead retired down the St Petersburg road. Some two or three leagues out of Smolensk two tracks branch off from the St Petersburg road and link it to that heading for Moscow. One of these minor roads passes behind Valutina, running close to Bredechino, whilst the other joins the Moscow road even further back, somewhere near the village of Slobnieva. Barclay now sought to re-join the Moscow road by means of either one of these tracks and had set his columns in motion. Ney hoped to intercept him and, by arriving at the Kolovdina defile and pushing through to the Valutina plateau, cut Barclay off from reaching his objective. No time was to be lost, for the Russians had realised the importance of this decisive moment, reinforcing their rearguard and selecting a position admirably suited to the defence. The terrain was boggy and treacherous and impeded the use of both artillery and infantry. The Moscow road passed over the Kolovdina stream by means of a bridge and then climbed the wooded heights, almost perpendicularly, before reaching the Valutina plateau. The Russians had placed infantry on this plateau and trained heavy guns on the road and on the valley below and had thrown thousands of light infantry into the surrounding woods. Ney did not have sufficient men with which to attack this formidable position and, initially, bombarded the Russians and sent forward clouds of skirmishers. However, just after five in the evening, Gudin's division of I Corps arrived, sent forward in support by the Emperor. Ney deployed and led his troops forward into the bloody battle.

Russian resistance was as stubborn as our attack was impetuous. They made every effort to win time for their troops to effect a retreat and were constantly reinforced by fresh troops. It was fortunate for them that Junot, off on their left flank, did not intervene against them. Assault followed assault, but, for the most part, they were unsuccessful and we suffered heavy casualties. Gudin himself fell at the head of his division, close by the Kolovdina bridge, struck down by a mortal wound. Only when III Corps' batteries arrived and, positioned on a height to the left of the main road, opened up a deadly fire did Ney lead his reserves forward to the attack. It was around 11 o'clock that evening, with the moon shining down on the heaps of bodies, that the Russians finally withdrew.

We camped where we stood on the field of battle, amongst the dead and wounded. Many of the latter dragged themselves towards our campfires, hoping to share in our meal. By the morning, most of these unfortunates had died.

37
IN CAMP BEFORE VALUTINA-GORA, 22 AUGUST

On the 20th, the day after the battle, we quitted the battlefield and made camp on the plateau, just to the right of the main road. Three days of rest followed, drawing to a close a bloody period of fighting.

We heard that we were to be reviewed by the Emperor, who had, the day after the fighting at Valutina, already reviewed Ney's other divisions and that of Gudin. Our days of rest were marked by the occasional return of a few inhabitants who had fled during the fighting. Some of them came over to our camp, meeting our curious troops who, by means of signs, gestures and a little Russian they had picked up, attempted to communicate with them.

38
BETWEEN DOROGOBOUYE AND SLAVKOVO, 27 AUGUST

After our three-day halt at Valutina-Gora, we broke camp on the 23rd and followed the Russian army, making arduous marches along the main road and braving the heat and enormous clouds of dust, and being jostled by swarms of other troops all struggling forward in the same direction.

Thus it was that, in the afternoon of the 26th, we reached Dorogobouye on the left bank of the Dnepr; this town was, like Smolensk and so many others, the victim of flames and was soon reduced to ashes. We only remained here a few hours, and camped a few miles further on, continuing our march, on the 27th, towards Viasma. Swarms of stragglers, who either could not keep up or who were charged with obtaining food, milled about and bore stark witness to the disorder besetting the army. The disappearance of the Jews and the oriental appearance of the architecture indicated that we were now gracing the soil of ancient Muscovy.

v. Pabor de Four gem: C. Küstner gedr.   Ensminger u. Baumaster lith.

39
SLAVKOVO, 27 AUGUST

Towards evening we passed an attractive country house, just off the main road and on the fringe of a wood. We distinctly heard music coming from this dwelling, the Slavkovo mansion, Napoleon's headquarters. The building, which was destroyed during the retreat, and the whole area around, were guarded by the Imperial Guard. Napoleon, in order to safeguard his ever-increasing lines of communication, sent an order out from here to Marshal Victor, on the Niemen, to advance to Smolensk with his corps, and send troops out to Mohilev and Vitebsk.

40
AROUND SEMLEVO, 28 AUGUST

On the 28th the army crossed the great plain of Viasma. We were advancing at speed, and infantry, cavalry and artillery were all mixed up and confused, pressing forward in the hope of a decisive battle at Viasma. Infantry and cavalry, in huge columns, marched on either side of the main road whilst the artillery, wagons and convoys covered the road itself.

The whole mass was shrouded in billowing dust, and we relied on a fleeting breeze to reveal who marched in front of us or behind us. More rarely still could we make out any distinguishing features in the surrounding countryside. Towards evening we reached Semlevo with its strangely constructed wooden church rising above the clouds of dust, reddening in the rays of the setting sun.

41
IN CAMP BEFORE VIASMA, 30 AUGUST

On the 28th Murat and Davout arrived before Viasma, a little town of 15,000 people and situated on the river of the same name. The Russians destroyed the bridges over the river during the night of the 28th and 29th, set fire to the town and withdrew towards Gjatsk, taking most of the town's population with them. At dawn on the 29th, Caulaincourt, making use of a ford, pushed into the town. Two battalions of the 25th Line followed and, after a supreme effort, managed to extinguish the fire and save some three-quarters of the town. That evening III Corps arrived at Viasma, after a difficult march across sandy terrain. We camped a little distance from the town and unable to see it because of a slight undulation in the terrain. It was only on the 30th, as we marched towards one of the bridges that had been repaired, that we caught sight of the town itself. It was lit up by the magnificent rays of the sun, which played on the golden domes of the oriental churches and convents, making them seem to rear up above the still-smoking ruins of burnt houses.

42
VIASMA, 30 AUGUST

On the morning of the 30th we marched through Viasma, part of which had been reduced to cinders. We had, in the last few days, caught sight of the Emperor more and more – something which always suggested an imminent battle – and we now came across him again, seated before a house in the eastern suburbs, surrounded by his staff and in conversation with a Russian nobleman as the troops marched past.

After a further hour and a half of marching, we made camp.

43
IN CAMP, 31 AUGUST

From Viasma onwards the land became more and more fertile, and our march through Gjatsk took us through rolling countryside and well-constructed villages. Most of these villages, which the Russians had not destroyed as they fell back before us, would soon be submerged under the torrent of the retreating French army and would disappear without trace.

Here we find III Corps, camped in the fields to the left of the main road, close by a stately country seat soon to become Marshal Ney's headquarters. The fields, cultivated with so much care, the houses, so clean and tidy, and the château, so charming and fine, all bore testament to the affluence and comfort of the inhabitants, all of whom had fled. Within one day of our arrival, all this prosperity had vanished, destroyed and trampled by our troops. By 1 September the charming scene depicted here had been entirely erased.

v. Faber du Faur del.

G. Kästner gedr.

Emminger u. Baumeister lith.

44
IN CAMP BEFORE GJATSK, 2 SEPTEMBER

We arrived at Gjatsk on the 1st and pitched camp not far from the town, on the edge of a pine forest. The entire army had concentrated around Gjatsk, having heard that Kutuzov had been appointed as commander of the Russian army – which suggested that they would offer battle. Our troops were granted a few days' rest in order to prepare for the inevitable confrontation and to reorganise our corps. This last measure was absolutely essential as our regiments, battalions and companies were, especially in III Corps, so seriously diminished. In their present condition, our units no longer made tactical sense. Thus it was that our three brigades barely furnished three battalions, namely one light battalion and two line battalions.

The two Portuguese regiments, which also fought in the ranks of II Corps, were pretty much in the same condition as us. Drawn from the westernmost extremity of Europe, and, by virtue of their stature and appearance, contrasting so markedly with our own troops, they seemed more African than European. They had crossed the Niemen at full strength, but had suffered terribly at Smolensk and Valutina and, more than perhaps any other unit, had suffered at the hands of the intemperate climate and the general want of everything. Their camp was adjoining ours and we could see just how few of them remained with their colours. Not long afterwards they almost disappeared altogether, swallowed up in the glorious assault on the Semenovskii redoubts and littering the field of Borodino with their dead. But few of them would see the ancient city of the Czars, with its magnificent domes, and fewer still would survive the first frosts, unaccustomed as they were to the glacial North. Perhaps none of them ever saw Lusitania again with its meadows in bloom and the paradise of the Guadiana, Tagus and Duro.

45
GJATSK, 4 SEPTEMBER

Imperial Headquarters left Gjatsk on the 4th and the army lurched forward towards Kolotskoi and Mojaisk. The departure of the troops meant that a little silence replaced the tumult of the last few days. But Gjatsk was not altogether deserted. After the reorganisation all the sick and wounded, and all those excluded from the ranks for whatever reason, remained, forming the new population of the town. The houses and streets were filled with life; here one could encounter men coming in from the surrounding camps seeking out houses; there others could be seen making themselves as comfortable as possible in their new quarters. Still others could be seen out and about, on the lookout for food and provisions, the lack of which they had been feeling for too long. Gjatsk seemed to be witnessing a very ordinary bustle – ordinary if it were not for the fact that the people were all attired in uniform. This fact was evidence, if any were needed, that the legions of the West were present in force and had inundated the soil of Russia.

This scene takes place in the west of Gjatsk, just where the Dorogobouye road enters the town. The architecture is quite typical of that of the region.

46
GJATSK, 5 SEPTEMBER

This peaceful interlude was of but brief duration. Two-thirds of this temporary population scarcely had time to settle in before being obliged to quit their lodgements. Fire took hold in the western portion of the town and, fanned by a stiff westerly wind, it made frightening progress and, in too short a space of time, had ravaged both the town's stone and wooden buildings. Carelessness, on the part of soldiers inexperienced in the art of heating and lighting houses constructed out of wood, was largely to blame. Nevertheless it was ironic that we had managed to extinguish a fire started by the Russians upon first entering the town: now, despite ourselves, we had managed to accomplish their task.

47
GJATSK, 5 SEPTEMBER

The road leading out of Gjatsk was closed off by a most singular looking barrier – a barrier painted in garish and outlandish colours. The sentry box was painted in a chequered pattern, the barrier's palisade in zigzags, in Russia's national colours. The barrier consisted of two mobile *chevaux-de-frise*, hinged so that they could swing open or remain closed according to circumstance. The barrier witnessed the movement of massive numbers of troops as it was through this gate, on the 4th and 5th, that the army's columns marched towards Borodino. It was an almost continual procession of soldiers of all kinds, and you could see men drawn from every nation of Europe jostling each other in their hurry to get to the fore.

48
NEAR GJATSK, 5 SEPTEMBER

Not far from this gate, in the direction of Mojaisk, we came across some elegant windmills; these reminded us of a Dutch or north German landscape rather than a Russian one. The area round about, however, was completely devoid of life as the army had swept on towards Kolotskoi and Borodino, steeling itself for the oncoming clash with Kutuzov. Only a few signs marked the passing of the great mass – dead horses, stragglers and cautious inhabitants emerging from their hideaways.

49
ON THE FIELD OF BORODINO, NEAR SEMENOVSKII, 7 SEPTEMBER

A long and bloody struggle was waged on the heights above the ruins of Semenovskii, for possession of the redoubts. Finally, towards noon, we secured the position after a combat of mixed success in which the redoubts were stormed, lost and stormed again. The redoubt on the right had fallen to the 25th Division as the battle raged at its fiercest. The enemy continually fed fresh troops into the fray and managed to turn back Murat's repeated charges. It was during one such reverse that Murat, pursued by enemy cuirassiers, sought shelter, so as not to fall into the hands of the enemy, in the redoubt taken by the 25th Division. Here, contrary to what Segur has written, he came upon steady troops fresh from having taken possession of the position after a bloody struggle and who were prepared to defend the place to the last. These were the troops who would earn for their marshal the title 'Prince of the Moskova' and win their general the title 'Count of the Empire'.

A vigorous fire from our light infantry, and from line infantry in their support, soon repulsed the enemy's cavalry and assured the safety of the King. He, Murat, threw himself upon the retreating foe with the cavalry of Bruyère and Nansouty and, after a number of attacks, forced them back off the heights.

50
NEAR VALUEVA, 8 SEPTEMBER

Borodino was fought with 120,000 men on each side and more than 1,000 pieces of artillery vomiting death and destruction the entire day. The Russians, pushed back from their positions and entrenchments, finally conceded defeat and withdrew from the field of battle soaked in the blood of more than 25,000 dead, whose bodies littered the field between Borodino and Semenovskii. And what were the fruits of victory? Virtually nil. Few trophies fell to the victors that bloody day – something that had characterised the campaign to date. Each army corps had triumphed, yet still we were cheated of a decisive victory. And we had sustained heavy casualties.

The Russian army had been beaten but not destroyed. It withdrew in good order and the victors, who had hoped to savour the fruits of a victory long-promised, including winter quarters and a prompt return to their homeland, found themselves suffering as much now as they had before the battle. Most of the victors would see the prize, Moscow; would see it ruined and in flames; would experience the cold and the frost of the retreat; and would perish in the icy fields of Russia.

The trophies were out of all proportion to the sacrifices we had made – some thirty guns, mostly taken in the redoubts, some of which were too badly damaged to be of service, and some 1,000 prisoners. These were our spoils!

The fate of these prisoners was terrible. Taken to Smolensk, they were dragged towards the Prussian frontier, tormented by hunger and deprived of even the most basic necessities, and almost all perished before leaving their native land.

51
ON THE FIELD OF BORODINO, 17 SEPTEMBER

Here, close by, in all its horror, was the valley of the Shevardino, close to where Morand's division had been positioned at the start of the battle. This is the battlefield long after the furious fighting had subsided, long after those violent passions had cooled, long after the powerful exclamations of honour and duty, which so stifle man's humanity, had died away. Now the battlefield has assumed the aspect we see before us, the ferocious masses of troops having been called away to some other scene of victory, and the silence of the tomb reigns supreme. Bodies lie in heaps, enemy and friend alike united in profound peace. Here and there a horse is still moving, having survived its deceased rider.

As we drew closer we could see that the corpses were, after eleven days, rotting away.

Below darkened skies, bands of fog, as though out of compassion, shielded us from seeing more of this vast scene of desolation. Even so, we could plainly see the blood-soaked contours of the grand redoubt, the possession of which had been contested with such unabated fury. A column had been erected within the redoubt bearing an inscription to the effect that here lay Montbrun and Caulaincourt, surrounded by fallen heroes.

The glory of our own troops was enshrined in these very redoubts, for it was here that Murat, overwhelmed by superior numbers, had sought shelter amongst us.

Here, on this field, we inscribed in the pages of history that never-to-be-forgotten name of Borodino. No struggle had ever been so stubbornly contested; none had seen such numbers employed or such casualties on such a restricted area.

52
THE BRIDGE OVER THE KOLOTSCHA, NEAR BORODINO VILLAGE, 17 SEPTEMBER

The bridge over the Kolotscha, situated just behind Borodino, was the scene of a bloody struggle on the 7th.

The battle had opened with the seizure of Borodino village. The 106th Line Regiment had been ordered to storm the village. Having done so, they charged on over the bridge, towards the Gorki heights. There, met by superior numbers, and confronted by a murderous fire from Russian entrenchments, they were thrown back to the bridge, having sustained terrible casualties. The 92nd Line were rushed to their support, saving the bridge from destruction.

During the battle the bridge had been cleared by throwing any corpses into the river. I saw that few now remained, hinting lightly at the terrible struggle that had taken place at this bridge over the Kolotscha.

53

BEHIND THE VILLAGE OF BORODINO, BY THE MAIN ROAD TO MOSCOW, 17 SEPTEMBER

Eleven days after the bloody battle we marched over the corpse-strewn field. Here the most horrific scenes lie far away in the distance and silence shrouds the countryside round about, for the angel of death had stalked this land.

Those who fought at Borodino will recognise the picture, drawn from the main Moscow road and looking back on the scene of destruction. On the right, in the valley where the Slonetz meets the Kolotscha, is Borodino village, the dome of its church looking down sadly on the ruins of Semenovskii to the left. It was here, between these two points, that the battle was fought; the fight was bitter but our troops were ultimately victorious.

54
ON THE MAIN ROAD BETWEEN MOJAISK AND KRYMSKOI, 18 SEPTEMBER

Crowds of wounded from both armies were scattered in countless villages after the battle of Borodino. Sooner or later these villages, either by chance or deliberately, burnt to the ground. It was then that these unfortunates, unable to flee on account of their wounds, found themselves at the mercy of the flames. It was not unusual to find charred corpses laid out on floors in serried lines. Those that survived, some horribly mutilated, sought some means to prolong their pitiful existence.

55
ON THE MAIN ROAD BETWEEN MOJAISK AND MOSCOW, 21 SEPTEMBER

As we advanced towards Moscow we passed through a number of villages, the houses of which strongly resembled Swiss houses in architecture and decoration. In addition, and going against the more usual custom of the country, each house had ornate glazed windows. The interiors of the houses also suggested a certain level of opulence and a sophistication hitherto lacking.

This was a sign, perhaps, that we were approaching the great city.

56
NINE LEAGUES FROM MOSCOW, TO THE RIGHT OF THE MAIN ROAD, 21 SEPTEMBER

As the army moved forward it left traces of its passage in its wake. This had been true after the battles of Smolensk and Valutina, but it was even more apparent after Borodino. Previously those who had been unable to follow the army had been either sick or too exhausted to go on; now the roads were clogged with the wounded and the dying. Those villages that lay on the main road between Kolotskoi and Moscow were choked with such unfortunates. Few of the wounded would survive for long; soon they would succumb to want of all kinds, or would die miserably in burning houses, or would fall under the blows of enraged peasants, bands of whom were roaming the area, or Kutuzov's Cossacks.

Here we find ourselves in a half-burnt village, just to the right of the main Moscow road, full to the brim with wounded or dismounted French hussars. Unable to grasp the danger of their situation, and too shortsighted in their temporary security, they refused our detachment a shelter for the night and rejoiced at our prompt departure. Those unfortunates! At dawn on the 22nd a strong force of Cossacks descended on the village and massacred all those who were unable to flee.

Peter de Flam del.   Gedr. von G. Kiechner   Kauffmann & Bennister lithogr.

57
ON THE MAIN ROAD BETWEEN MOJAISK AND MOSCOW, 22 SEPTEMBER

The following incident goes to show that luck and chance occasionally play a part in saving men from even the most pressing dangers.

The artillery reserve of the 25th Division, reinforced by soldiers released from hospital or lightly wounded at Borodino, was to the rear of the army. We were still in the habit of sending men forward to arrange quarters for the coming night, to prepare lodgings on, or close by, the route we were to follow. We followed this procedure on the 21st and sent forward our depot, aiming to establish quarters in a village and château just off the main road. However, when our troops arrived they found themselves confronted by a strong detachment of French carabiniers and these men would not allow our men to establish themselves. The same thing happened in a number of other villages until, finally, after much trouble, our men discovered a tiny, abandoned village. We took possession of this at once and it was fortunate we did so as the château and other villages were raided by enemy cavalry at dawn the following day and all who could not flee were sabred or carried off as prisoners. Our artillery reserve, moving forward to catch up with the depot, heard the sound of firing and soon collided with fleeing carabiniers, dragoons and hussars, riding hell for leather and pursued by enemy cavalry.

Meanwhile, the same fate would have befallen our depot had not a battalion of the Old Guard and some artillery, all commanded by a general, arrived in the village. The general had realised the danger, halted his troops and fought off the enemy. The depot now moved off under the protection of this battalion and some convalescents, heading for a forest through which the Moscow road ran.

58
EIGHT LEAGUES FROM MOSCOW, TO THE LEFT OF THE MAIN ROAD, 23 SEPTEMBER

Our march through this forest was obstructed by a mass of wagons and fugitives compelled to halt after having encountered Cossacks amongst the trees. We came to a standstill, something made necessary by the firing to our front and shots coming from off to our right. As we halted, the fugitives seized the opportunity to attach themselves to our convoy and other trains soon swelled our ranks, amongst them an Italian artillery train. Our convoy soon numbered over one hundred wagons.

von Faber du Faur gez.   G. Küstner gedr.   Emminger u. Baumeister lith.

59
EIGHT LEAGUES FROM MOSCOW,
TO THE LEFT OF THE MAIN ROAD,
23 SEPTEMBER

Towards noon the firing died away and our scouts reported that no enemy could be discovered in the vicinity. We moved off, forming our wagons into two lines and protected by the Guard battalion serving as skirmishers.

We passed the night of the 22nd to 23rd in this position, cautious and fearing that our column presented too exposed a target. On the morning of the 23rd we caught sight of two long lines of enemy cavalry off to our right. However, as we were reinforced by the arrival of some dragoons and Guard lancers, the enemy settled for some rather insignificant skirmishing. In the evening the enemy veered off to the right, but not before sending some Cossacks against us. Firing again broke out in the forest. The enemy was so well received by the Guard battalion and by the convalescents of the 25th Division that they were beaten off and disappeared over the horizon. As night fell our troops received the order to make their way to Moscow. It was raining, a factor which aided our enterprise, and on the 24th, early in the morning, we arrived, safe and sound, in Moscow. The rest of the convoy, which had held back to see whether or not we had been successful, delayed rather too long and was ambushed on the way.

60
MOSCOW, 24 SEPTEMBER

On the 14th our troops had made their way over the heights before Moscow. From there they looked down on the thousand golden domes of the magnificent city of the Czars. In the centre of the city we could see the Kremlin. The city was shrouded in silence; a mute canvas lay before us. No smoke rose from the city's chimneys, no curious inhabitants came to stare at the victorious foreigners, no deputation came to implore mercy from the vanquishers. Moscow, just like Smolensk, Dorogobouye, Viasma and others before it, had been abandoned by its inhabitants and Murat, with his cavalry corps, trailing the Russian rearguard through the city's streets, heard nothing but the echo of his horses' hooves.

Our arrival was the signal for the fire. On the night of the 14th to 15th the Russians set fire to a number of areas but seemed to concentrate on the shops in the Chinese quarter. Despite every effort to put out the conflagration, the fire raged until the 19th, and on the 20th the catastrophe was complete. Two-thirds of the city's buildings were now nothing more than heaps of ashes. Moscow became the grave of our every hope. There was an odious and penetrating smell of burning infecting the air; tracts of land contained nothing more than rubble and ashes, collapsed roofs and corpses. Few areas had escaped from the fire and perhaps only the Kremlin, and a handful of suburbs, along with a number of palaces, churches and monasteries, had been spared and served as oases in this desert of ash.

Here and there groups of unfortunate inhabitants could be seen wandering in the grim labyrinth, hoping to discover that some part of their home had escaped destruction or to dig up some miserable food in order to prolong their unhappy existence. Our troops were everywhere, hoping to discover some trophy and, like children, satisfy their greed with some bauble, only to discard it as soon as they came across some other novelty. Few – too few – took the opportunity to prepare themselves for the encroaching Russian winter. That which was valuable or useful was soon squandered, and order was only restored when it was too late, detachments being sent into the city with specific orders to procure necessities and supplies.

61
GUARDING III CORPS' ARTILLERY PARK, BY THE VLADIMIR GATE, MOSCOW, 2 OCTOBER

III Corps' artillery park was situated by the Vladimir Gate and was guarded by Württemberg, French and Dutch troops. Soon, however, the position was deemed vulnerable and the park was relocated in a square, with sentries being lodged in a merchant's house close by. The rest of III Corps' artillery were quartered a short distance from the park.

Here we see the park's sentries at their posts. Cold nights and mornings had already led to the troops' adopting some strange costumes: one of the sentries, a Dutch gunner, keeps out the cold with a fur cap, warms his hands in a muff and, under his greatcoat, sports a nightgown. Such precautions were but the prelude to the universal adoption of attempts to keep out the cold.

62
THE CHURCH OF THE OLD BELIEVERS, MOSCOW, 3 OCTOBER

III Corps' artillery were quartered in the Military Academy, a building in the Lafertovskaja district on the left bank of the Jausa by the Soltikov bridge, throughout our stay in Moscow.

The surrounding area was magnificent, covered in trees and presenting a delightful appearance. Exploring the area, we came across a beautiful church, hidden in a charming clump of trees. It was a most dazzling sight: its cupolas were blue and speckled with golden stars and towered forth over the brilliant masses of autumnal leaves. This was the Church of the Old Believers, although I was unable to discover whether it was actually frequented by Old Believers or whether it was just named after them.

63
SIMONOV MONASTERY, MOSCOW, 7 OCTOBER

To the south of the city, not far from the Officers' College and close by the Powder Magazine, is the Simonov Monastery. As with other Russian monasteries, it is fortified, encircled by a charming turreted wall. Whilst we were in Moscow it served as a depot for dismounted cavalry, and, if I am not very much mistaken, it fell victim to flames as we were preparing to leave the city.

64
MOSCOW, 8 OCTOBER

Picture yourself on the north-west bastion of the Powder Magazine as the sun is setting. From here you look down on an area ravaged by flames, in the centre of which is one of Moscow's hundreds of beautiful churches, buildings remarkable for their style and infinite colour. The church had been spared from the flames thanks to its solid construction, sound roof and the lack of combustible materials within. Perhaps, too, religious piety had prevented the incendiaries from attempting to set such temples on fire. Through radiant autumnal trees and light mist can be seen buildings in the Kolomenskaya Sloboda along with others in the Paetniskaya quarter. The tanneries were located in the Serpuchovskaya district, between the Treasury and the Semlaenoi-Gorod.

65
MOSCOW, 8 OCTOBER

The most imposing view from the bastion of the Powder Magazine was undoubtedly that to the south-east. This is a portion of that spectacular view. Behind the ruins of the Krutizkaya Sloboda rise the walls of the Krutizkaya Podvorye, which, before the fire, had served as a barracks for gendarmes. Behind this, and separated from it by a ravine and the Sarra stream, is the Novo Spatskoi Monastery with its superb bell-tower (the second largest in Moscow, after the Ivan the Terrible tower in the Kremlin). On the extreme right lies the Pokrovskoi Monastery, its towers surrounded by a veritable forest of fruit trees.

On the left can be seen the Paetniskaya Palace and jetties on the right bank of the Moskova, as well as buildings of the Jauskaya district on the left bank.

66
IN THE VICINITY OF LAFERTOVSKAJA SLOBODA, MOSCOW, 11 OCTOBER

If you stand on the left bank of the Jausa, between the Military Academy and the Church of the Old Believers, with your back to the latter, you look out towards the Soltikov bridge and the road which runs between the German Quarter and the Vladimir Gate. The banks of the river are tree-lined, and these trees partially obscure the Military Hospital and the Lafertovskaja suburb. To the left can be seen a group of buildings occupied by Imperial Quarters and a number of the 25th Division's officers.

Fabre del Faur pinx.   gedr. von J. Velten   Emminger lith.

67
MOSCOW, 11 OCTOBER

There was a particularly beautiful church, a little distance from the German Quarter, in the direction of the Kremlin. It was remarkable chiefly on account of its multitude of bell-towers and had, by and large, escaped the flames, standing out from the desolation that surrounded it. It took us some time to learn the name of the street, and the identity of the saint to whom this richly coloured church was consecrated. There were too few inhabitants around to ask, and those that remained would flee as soon as they caught sight of us. The street itself was so littered with debris that it was impossible to get from one end to the other.

Finally, by dint of persistence, I learned that the street was called Basmannaya and that the church was under the protection of Saint Nicetas.

68
SUMMER (OR IMPERIAL) GARDEN, MOSCOW, 16 OCTOBER

In the eastern part of Moscow, close by the German Quarter and the Imperial Palace, was situated the Summer, or Imperial, Garden, divided into two parts by the Jausa. It was one of the most delightful parts of the city, with graceful bowers, isles and bridges, the whole surrounded by palaces.

69
IN THE KREMLIN, MOSCOW, 17 OCTOBER

Moscow boasts hundreds of churches, resplendent with gold, silver and brightly coloured, shimmering domes, earning for its city, the ancient capital of the Czars, the title of the City of the Golden Cupolas. It is an astonishing sight, the only one of its kind, perhaps, in the entire world. The city is a wonder to behold in the sunlight, particularly as you emerge from the forests to the west of Moscow, on the Mojaisk road.

From the midst of these golden domes rises the Kremlin, which, besides the Czar's Palace, the Arsenal and the Patriarch's Residence, held within its walls more than thirty churches. Two of the churches, of especial significance on account of their antiquity, purpose, architecture and relics contained within, were close to the Czar's Palace. One, with nine golden cupolas and a roof fashioned in the same style, was adjacent to the Palace and, for that reason, was called the Church of the Court; this was the Cathedral of the Annunciation. The other temple had five silver cupolas and was where Czars were crowned. It was the Cathedral of the Assumption.

The Cathedral of the Annunciation was founded in 1397 by Grand Duke Vasili Dmitrieivitch and completed ten years later. It was demolished a little later, but restoration began in 1484 during the reign of Ivan Vasilivitch and the church was reopened in 1489. In 1697 and 1770 Peter the Great and Catherine the Great, respectively, restored the interior.

The Cathedral of the Assumption was founded in 1325 by Peter, Metropolitan of Kiev, and was completed in 1327. Struck by lightning in 1492, it was rebuilt in 1519 by Grand Duke Ivan Ivanovitch. The interior was decorated by gold-leaf frescos commissioned by Czar Ivan Feodorovitch in 1692, and Catherine II restored the church in 1773.

In October 1812 the square to the east of the church was covered with hundreds of French and Allied caissons which, owing to the lack of draught horses, had been deposited within the Kremlin's walls. The square was so congested that it was in fact rather difficult to find a suitable position from which to draw.

The caissons were abandoned when we commenced our retreat and gunpowder from them was later used for blasting mine galleries beneath the Kremlin.

a Paris chez Bance ainé.

G. Arnout imp.

F. Benoist del.

70
MOSCOW, 18 OCTOBER

During our stay in Moscow, the tomb of our hopes, those few inhabitants remaining in the city kept well away from us, as though we carried some contagious disease. They hid in the ruins or in churches and spent their days, like us, in worry and care, hoping for better days to come.

When, however, Murat was surprised and beaten at Tarutino by the wily Kutuzov, victory now seeming to smile on the Russians for the first time, news of these events caused joy to the inhabitants. As we became discouraged, new hope was born amongst the Russians.

71
AT THE KALUGA GATE, MOSCOW, 19 OCTOBER

The Emperor had busied himself with preparations for our departure for a good number of days. The sick and wounded were despatched towards Mojaisk and Smolensk, those too ill to make the journey being placed in the Foundling Hospital to be cared for by the army's medical personnel. Dismounted cavalry, to the number of 4,000 men, were organised into four battalions. Army corps were passed in review by the Emperor; it was the turn of the Imperial Guard and, on the 18th, that of Ney's divisions. As these latter were being reviewed, news arrived that Murat had been surprised and had sustained heavy losses around Vinkovo. The review was, it is true, completed, but, as we filed out of the Kremlin heading for our quarters in the German Quarter, we received orders to quit Moscow the following day. Thus it was that on the 19th we set out on the march that would result in the annihilation of the entire army. The troops were set in motion before dawn and, keeping the Young Guard and the four battalions of dismounted cavalry in the Kremlin as a rearguard under Mortier, filed out of the city through the Kaluga Gate. The streets were crowded – in fact stuffed fit to burst – as corps ran into corps. Time after time the way was blocked by disorganised convoys, for 500 guns, 2,000 wagons, drawn by exhausted horses, and countless carts and vehicles of all types and from all nations, loaded with booty or supplies, accompanied the army and slowed it down.

The sun was high in the sky on this fine autumnal day when, after considerable effort, we finally reached the Kaluga Gate. We halted here, waiting in vain for two of our guns. These guns had got lost in the crowded streets and only re-joined us a few hours later.

72
ON THE ROAD FROM MOSCOW TO KALUGA, NEAR BYKASSOVO, 23 OCTOBER

Overcoming a number of difficulties, in part caused by our horses dropping from exhaustion and in part from the disorder reigning in the marching columns, we finally pushed through the Desna and Krasnaya-Pakra defiles and, on 24 October, reached Czirikovo. We then left the old Kaluga road, turning off to the right in order to gain, via Rudnevo, the new road. As we made this oblique march we found ourselves bogged down in clay soil churned up by the rain, and it was here that we began to lose wagons, horses and caissons. We had been able to reach Czirikovo without any such loss, but it had only been after a supreme effort and now our horses were exhausted. From now on we abandoned or destroyed what we could not haul with us. We even had to leave behind some of the more exhausted horses. The rearguard burnt any wagons it came across so that they would no fall into enemy hands. Sometimes soldiers did not even wait for the rearguard to come up but attempted to destroy vehicles then and there, placing the troops marching past in extreme danger. Here, for example, as some artillerymen attempt to rid themselves of a caisson, a mounted gendarme rides up and fires his pistol at it in order to set it ablaze. It explodes, costing the gendarme his life and burning a number of men most horribly. These would die a miserable death but a few days later as the march continued.

von Faber du Faur gem.　　　　　　　　　C. Kästner gedr.　　　　　　　　　E. Eigninger u. Baumeister lith.

73
BEFORE BOROVSK, 26 OCTOBER

After considerable effort, and constantly being hustled forward by our rearguard, we reached Borovsk on the 25th just as night was falling. Here we made camp and found that most of the army had done likewise, but the town and a number of villages around were on fire; this, combined with the sea of campfires, transformed a mellow autumnal evening into a scene of awful grandeur.

On the morning of the 26th large bands of Cossacks attacked those villages that lined the Moscow road and killed, wounded or chased out those stragglers who had lodged there. Next they attempted to attack the army's camps, but a few discharges of cannon and a charge of Guard cavalry drove them off. Nevertheless, they were visibly encouraged by our evident disorder, and these horsemen now grew far bolder than they had been at the beginning of the campaign.

It was here, at Borovsk, that fortune seemed to turn her back on us. Here we received news of Malojaroslavets and, shortly afterwards, the order that we should march on Mojaisk, via Vereya, and re-join the Moscow–Smolensk road. This we began to do on the afternoon of the 26th, even though it took us away from a region untouched by the hand of war and brought us back on to a road which had been transformed into a desert strewn with the dead and the dying even during our first passage. This was the start of the retreat proper, and the event that signalled the destruction of the entire army. We were promised comfortable winter quarters in Smolensk, amongst its richly provisioned stores and magazines. But we were eighteen days' march away from those stores – eighteen days at the mercy of hunger, the climate and our enemies!

74
BETWEEN DOROGOBOUYE AND MIKALEVKA, 7 NOVEMBER

The order had been given for us to turn off the Kaluga road and make our way to the Smolensk–Moscow road. Up until that point, despite the numerous difficulties we had encountered along near impassable roads – difficulties that often led to losses of men, horses and caissons – we had, at least, always managed to find some food. We had, too, always marched as a disciplined body and had not lost a gun, despite fighting in some particularly bloody engagements. But now we found ourselves in a land already stripped by both ourselves and our enemies.

Even so, we still hoped to reach Smolensk before the furies of winter fell upon us – Smolensk, where we would find well-stocked magazines and shelter, where Victor and his corps, placed in reserve, would bid us a warm welcome. Therefore, led by our hope, we traversed the field of Borodino, marched through Gjatsk and, on the 3rd, pushed through the Russians at Viasma. However, on the 5th and 6th the sky grew overcast and there were occasional flurries of snow. On the 7th a massive snowstorm robbed us of the day and announced the true arrival of the Russian winter. We struggled forward, unsure of where we were or who surrounded us. The furious storm blew huge flakes of ice into our faces – flakes which soon settled and sought to obstruct our march. The horses found the going difficult on the icy surface and gave up. Convoys and, for the first time, cannon were abandoned. The road began to be littered with frozen bodies, and these, soon covered with a snowy winding sheet, formed small mounds. This was all that was to remain of so many of our comrades-in-arms.

The Russian winter finished off what starvation, exhaustion and retreat had been unable to accomplish. The army disbanded and melted away. Now it resembled a rabble – men of all arms, of all army corps, marching in small bands or alone. They had not deliberately abandoned their flags, but cold and an instinct for self-preservation made men quit their units. Continuing the march was a terrible effort every single day; for the gunners it was especially tough as they tried to look after their horses and save their guns. The most terrible part, though, was the night – sixteen hours of darkness, camped in the snow, without food, without a fire. The first such winter camp was that at Mikalevka, on the night of the 7th.

75
CAMP NEAR MIKALEVKA, 7 NOVEMBER

The fatal retreat had begun. The ancient city of the Czars was nothing but a heap of smouldering rubble and eyes had turned westwards towards far-off homelands. Whilst the sky had been serene and our feet trod upon firm earth, all had gone well. Our thin garments had protected us from autumnal breezes, we found food in villages, and the soldiers, even when suffering, had hope of better things to come. But the sky clouded over, the snow fell and the icy North came down upon us with all its attendant furies. The road disappeared and, for as far as one could see, a sheet of white stretched to the horizon. The faithful gunners made incredible efforts to save their pieces; they buried those they could no longer drag with them.

After a day in which we had suffered as never before, we reached a village and came across some snow-covered huts. Some of our comrades had preceded us and sought out shelter for us. But all was quiet and we assumed they had now abandoned the huts and resumed their march. As we drew nearer, however, we came across corpses frozen stiff and saw in their fate our own destiny. We sought to brace ourselves for all the future could hurl against us, but the sinister end to the first day of winter marked but the start of our woe.

76
ON THE ROAD, NOT FAR FROM PNEVA, 8 NOVEMBER

From Mikalevka, where we spent the night, the retreat continued the following day. The brilliant army that had crossed the Niemen would scarcely recognise itself now. The cold had deprived us of our brilliance and our clothes were as those of a sorry troop of adventurers. The man on the left, the most brilliant captain, seems oblivious to the group warming their hands by a fire fed by broken wheels and gun carriages. Behind them stand the ordnance officers, ready for the least signal. Do you recognise the man dressed in the simple grey overcoat? The man who led us so often in battle and to victory now partially disguised in a fur cap? It is the Emperor. Who knows what must be going through his mind as his pitiful army files past? His enemies have insulted him and tarnished his glory. Oh, cruel torture! But those who cast their eyes on fallen grandeur momentarily forget their own suffering, and thus it was that we filed past in mournful silence, partially reconciled to our terrible fate.

77
IN THE SUBURBS OF SMOLENSK,
ON THE RIGHT BANK OF THE BORYSTHENE,
12 NOVEMBER

We arrived at Smolensk after twenty days' marching. We had marched through this town in triumph only two and a half months before, but now we entered it covered in rags. We had redoubled our efforts to reach this place, borne by hope of rest and succour. But our illusions were soon shattered. There was no food, no clothing – not even a shelter from the rigours of the cold. Here the final binds of order and discipline were cast aside; from now on we thought of ourselves alone and sought to prolong our own existence.

At Smolensk we broke up the last of our gun carriages, dragged here with so much effort. We threw the barrels into the Dnepr. Imagine the despair of the poor gunner who, having sworn to remain true to his gun, now has to cast it aside having survived together through so many hazards of war.

78
CAMP IN SMOLENSK, 13 NOVEMBER

So here we were in the promised land of Smolensk, a place where we thought to put an end to our suffering, the goal of our every effort. We had imagined abundance in the city's depots, warm houses to accommodate us and secure winter quarters to end our woe. All this had maintained our courage and kept the soldiers in the ranks. But it was all a lie. It was nothing more than a miserable pit, and Smolensk, instead of putting an end to the destruction, merely hastened the end of the entire army.

We established our camp in eighteen degrees of frost, in the midst of the burnt ruins of a house. We had but little food, and that had had to be snatched from magazines surrounded by spectres maddened by hunger. This is all Smolensk, that great city, had to offer.

We had to continue the march through the cold and horror. And the frontier of Russia was another thirty days' march away! We destroyed a number of guns here and, pooling our resources, found the means to drag with us four 6-pounders – all that remained of our artillery. We placed our sick and dying in houses in the New Square, for these had been converted into hospitals. These hospitals could not deal with such a scale of suffering and they presented a horrifying spectacle. The unfortunate sick were scattered here and there, in amongst the columns of the arcades or still slumbering in the wagons that had brought them here. Abandoned by everyone, deprived of all care, the vast majority fell victim to the cold of the first night.

Whilst in Smolensk we heard the rumble of guns – a noise that announced the arrival of Kutuzov's Russians.

79
BETWEEN KORYTHNIA AND KRASNOI, 15 NOVEMBER

At five o'clock in the morning of 14 November, Imperial Headquarters and the Imperial Guard left Smolensk. Four hours later what remained of the 25th Division followed. There were just a couple of hundred combatants left in its ranks, although a brigade of 200 men remained behind to form part of the rearguard under Marshal Ney. We also had four guns and a confused crowd of thousands of unarmed and strangely dressed fugitives, numbers of horses and all kinds of transport. No sooner had we passed through the city's gates than our losses began to mount; one of our gun carriages collapsed and we had to abandon the piece.

We dragged ourselves through deep snow, leaving traces of our passage in our wake. We made our way painfully as far as Korythnia, which we reached at nightfall, and we spent the night there. On the 15th we resumed our march towards Krasnoi. Towards noon we heard the noise of explosions; at first we took this to be the noise of caissons being destroyed, but it soon became apparent that it was the noise of cannon. We soon learned that it was the Russians attacking the Imperial Guard, for, now, we too suffered the same fate. Suddenly, through the snow, we saw a huge cloud of Cossacks flood on to the road ahead. Simultaneously, masses of infantry, cavalry and artillery appeared on our left. When they were no more than 4,500 paces from us they opened fire, sending a murderous discharge of round shot and grape against us. These were Miloradovich's 20,000 Russians, and they had occupied Krasnoi in order to cut our retreat.

80
BETWEEN KORYTHNIA AND KRASNOI, 15 NOVEMBER

We advanced, benefiting from the cover afforded by some pine trees that lined the road, and, despite our enfeebled state, fired back with our three guns. We were only able to get off a couple of shots before our pieces were silenced by the overwhelming fire of the enemy artillery. Now we prepared ourselves to fight our way through the enemy barring our way and link up with the Imperial Guard. We buried our guns so that they would not fall into the hands of the Cossacks, formed ourselves up into a column, with the armed men to the fore, and advanced. The Russians did not wait to resist our attack but moved out of the way, whilst Miloradovich's men were content to shadow us on our left and bring their artillery to bear against us. Of course, Miloradovich could have captured every last one of us with even a tenth of his troops. Eventually we arrived at Krasnoi, having sustained some loss but having come through the enemy.

81
CAMP AT KRASNOI, 16 NOVEMBER

We had forced our way through the Russians and reached Krasnoi as night fell. The Young Guard, under Mortier, was stationed on the road to Korythnia whilst Imperial Headquarters and the Old Guard, which still counted some 5,000 men in its ranks, occupied the little town and filled every house. Everyone else, including ourselves, had to make do with whatever shelter they could find in the streets and gardens and considered themselves lucky if they were able to warm themselves by a fire. This is how we spent the night. We awoke on the morning of the 16th and only then did we appreciate the losses of the day before – men were missing, equipment and *matériel* lost – and the danger we were now in as Kutuzov's 90,000 Russians had cut all apparent means of escape. Before us the road to Gadi was occupied by Russians, the bulk of their army lay on our left flank and Miloradovich was on the Krasnoi–Korythnia road, barring our retreat to Smolensk and preventing us from linking up with Eugène, Ney and Davout, whose troops still lay around that town. However, we were not disheartened for we placed our confidence in Napoleon and were convinced that, however we might fare against the Russian climate, we were more than equal to the Russian troops.

We spent the whole of the 16th waiting for the three army corps to come up from Smolensk and making demonstrations against the Russians around Krasnoi. The boom of cannon and the rattle of musketry resounded around this little town throughout the day. During the night of 16/17 November the Guard managed to extricate Eugène and the remains of his corps. But as Ney and Davout had not appeared by noon on the 17th, and fearing that we had remained too long at Krasnoi, and that the defile to Orscha might be cut, we began to march off towards Lyadi. Thus the Imperial Guard marched out of Krasnoi and attacked the Russians to our left; these quickly fell back. All of a sudden all firing stopped and we were able to reach Lyadi without hindrance and without having seen or heard the enemy.

82
NEAR BOBR, 23 NOVEMBER

Although there had been something of a thaw over the last couple of days, this was soon replaced by heavy snow – something that impeded our march. Russian columns shadowed us, but at a distance as they too were suffering from the intemperate climate. However, we were still surrounded by clouds of Cossacks and bands of armed peasants, and this made it very dangerous to stray from the main road or lag behind.

Here we see a typical scene – something that happened every day. A wounded officer and his wife, after considerable efforts to get this far, have just seen the horse pulling their sledge collapse and die. The bulk of the army has already passed by but there is still some hope that the rearguard might be able to assist them. But night is approaching and the rearguard is some way off – the smoke in the distance is a sign that it has just left a village and has set it on fire. The Cossacks appear. The compassion and bravery of a handful of soldiers serves as some encouragement for the unlucky pair but they are now without transport and if the rearguard does not take pity on them they will be abandoned and captivity will follow. Either that or they will perish, victims of the murderous climate.

83
CAMP AT STUDIANKA, 26 NOVEMBER

We left our camp at Nimanitschi before dawn on the 26th and marched for Borisov with the rest of the army; Borisov had fallen to Chichagov on the 23rd but had been recaptured by the Duke of Reggio on the 24th. Night had fallen by the time we reached the town. We then followed the river for two leagues, the glow of the Russian campfires on the right bank helping us in our progress. When day broke our march was masked by a forest of pines. Firing could be heard but it seemed distant and muffled; however, it grew louder that afternoon. It was Oudinot, who, with II Corps, had crossed the river and was pushing Chichagov back towards Borisov.

We reached Studianka, which lies at the foot of some heights, that evening. The heights had guns positioned on them to defend the bridges that had been thrown across the river by General Eblé on the morning of the 26th. The bridge on the right was designed for infantry and cavalry whilst that a little further downstream was intended for artillery and all kinds of other vehicles.

The river itself is quite wide, with marshy banks, and is about six feet deep. There were ramps serving as approaches to the bridges, but these were partially flooded as the water level had risen recently. Wood from the village had been used to build the bridges, and what remained had largely been consumed in the campfires. What little was left served as our shelter that night whilst we waited to cross the river. The place was so crowded that we thought ourselves lucky to find shelter from the glacial winds against the walls of a hut and next to the headquarters of the French gendarmes.

84
ON THE RIGHT BANK OF THE BERESINA, 27 NOVEMBER

At two in the morning of the 27th the Guard and III Corps, including the 25th Division – which, from six regiments of infantry, four cavalry regiments and 1,000 artillerymen, could now scarcely muster 150 men and no guns – broke camp and crossed the bridges to the right bank. All those officers who no longer had men to command followed this movement five hours later. This was a signal for the masses of fugitives camped on the left bank to throw themselves towards the bridges. Dawn saw a confused crowd of men, horses and vehicles pour down towards the bridges, almost as though they were attempting to carry them by assault. Although the enemy was still some distance off, the situation was frightening and the horror of it all was augmented by orders given to the gendarmes and pontonniers not to let anyone pass but armed men or those in formation. All others were pushed back into the crowd, most often by force, and hundreds were crushed underfoot or thrust into the water. Even those who were granted permission to cross the bridges were not entirely out of danger. If they managed to negotiate the slippery ramps they were lucky, but, from there onwards, if they chanced to slip they would certainly be trampled underfoot or pushed into the icy waters of the Beresina.

In the midst of the confusion stood the Emperor. He was close by the riverbank, between the two bridges, and he sought to exert some measure of order over the chaos around him. He oversaw the crossing until the evening when, with his suite, he himself made his way to the right bank and established his headquarters in the hamlet of Zaniviki.

The majority of our men camped as soon as they got to the right bank. Ignoring everything around them, they thought of nothing but lighting a fire, cooking and warming themselves. Cruel fate! The gusts of snow were so violent that night that it was almost impossible to keep a fire burning. We ourselves had just managed to melt a little snow for drinking water when IX Corps arrived, hustled us out of our camp and obliged us to seek shelter further on.

85
CAMP ON THE RIGHT BANK OF THE BERESINA, 27 NOVEMBER

Forced to abandon our fire, we wandered off in the direction of Zaniviki. We arrived there in the pitch dark with thick snow everywhere. Imperial Headquarters was based here, as was the Guard and a mass of troops and stragglers attracted by the glow of campfires. All the houses were occupied, and it was only after considerable effort, and some hard searching, that we found a house occupied by our staff, officers and soldiers. We had to obtain some wood at gunpoint to feed our fire, and we settled down for the night in the deep snow. There was no food. Soon fighting broke out – not, as one might expect, for room inside the houses but for the houses themselves: the soldiers, maddened by the cold, had clambered onto the roofs and started to demolish the houses for wood. The occupiers fought vainly to prevent this but, by the following morning, Zaniviki had disappeared, consumed by countless campfires.

Meanwhile, as night fell, the crowds of people who had not crossed on the 27th grew silent. They settled down among the ruins of Studianka, along the heights or in amongst the mass of wagons and vehicles now forming an immense and virtually impenetrable ring around the bridges. Campfires illuminated the entire area. The majority of these unfortunates, worn down by their privations, had grown insensible to suffering or believed themselves protected by Victor's corps, the left flank of which had taken up position on the Studianka heights.

Thus it was that the night of the 27th passed by. Artillery fire, which broke out on both banks simultaneously, heralded the dawn of the 28th. Wittgenstein, with 40,000 Russians, was bearing down upon us from the direction of Borisov, whilst Chichagov, with 27,000 men, was attempting to attack the bridges on the right bank. For most of the unfortunates on the left bank the final hour had come. They rose up and threw themselves towards the bridges. The bridge on the left, intended for guns and wagons, collapsed for the third time under the weight of the fugitives, and any attempt to repair it was frustrated by the subsequent disorder and confusion.

A single idea took hold of the crowd, a single objective: to reach the bridge. And in order to do so the fugitives were prepared to crush every obstacle and force their way past anyone, be it friend, commander, woman or child. People were thrust into the freezing waters of the Beresina or pushed into the flames of the burning house between the two bridges.

Victor, his corps now reduced to 6,000 men, made heroic efforts to stem Wittgenstein's advance, whilst Oudinot, Ney and Dombrowski managed to push Chichagov back on Stakova. Even so, Wittgenstein, with vastly superior numbers, was gradually pushing Victor back towards the bridges, so much so that he was able to bring artillery fire to bear on the crowds of fugitives struggling to reach the crossing. The desperation of this mass reached fever pitch. Each Russian shell or round shot found a target, and swathes of unfortunates were cut down. The cries of the multitude muffled the sound of the artillery as they made a supreme effort. In a convulsed wave they surged forward, crushing the dead and the dying underfoot. Finally night fell and the Russian artillery fire first grew sporadic before ceasing altogether. Towards nine in the evening Victor's corps forced a passage through a scene of desolation and passed over to the right bank, leaving a rearguard in Studianka.

A good number of unfortunates failed to take the opportunity of crossing with relative ease and on the morning of the 29th woke to find the Russians advancing and a vast crowd milling around the bridges. It was all for nothing as, at 8.30, the bridges were set on fire and all means of crossing the river went up in flames. The same fate would have befallen all those who had crossed over to the right bank had Chichagov destroyed the series of bridges which spanned the marshes between Zaniviki and Zembin. Fortunately, he failed to realise the importance of this defile and we arrived at Zembin having ourselves destroyed the bridges and placed the marsh between ourselves and the pursuing enemy.

87
BETWEEN PLESZENITZY AND SMORGONI, 2 DECEMBER

The Beresina was behind us and we were happy to have marched over the series of bridges over the Zembin marshes. Vilna, with its magazines and stores, was now the object of our attention. Those who could outstrip the army were sometimes lucky enough to find shelter in inhabited places. Here we see some officers of the 25th Division in the room of a farmhouse; they probably still remember their pretty hostess who went by the name of The Carpenter's Wife.

88
NEAR SMORGONI, 3 DECEMBER

During the first few days of December the cold increased tremendously and the dissolution of the army was almost completed. Those few detachments that had crossed the Beresina in good order now dissolved, and the roads we moved on were, more and more, covered with the corpses of men and horses, victims of hunger, exhaustion and, above all, the deadly cold. The sick and the dying were soon stripped of their clothing by those that followed behind and buried under the snow. Smolensk had been our great hope but now it was Vilna. There we hoped to find enough to satisfy our needs and protection afforded by the numerous troops of the garrison. Vilna would be our winter quarters. We were prepared to sacrifice our last drop of energy to reach Vilna.

We arrived at Smorgoni at noon on the 3rd. There we met 1,600 replacements for our division, waiting patiently for us in this small town. But the division was no more and, before long, the replacements met the same fate. Assigned to the rearguard, they soon vanished after a couple of nights in the cold. Those few who survived were in a pitiful condition by the time we reached Vilna, and we now saw what would befall any such reserves attempting to join us.

89
NEAR OSCHIMANY, 4 DECEMBER

The cold was getting worse and we were losing more and more men and horses. Many soldiers who had survived numerous campaigns and suffering of every description now succumbed to the cold. As we headed for Vilna we were reinforced by depots and reserves. But it was all for nothing: their support was transient and served only to augment our casualties. Thrust from their comfortable quarters, most of these young troops, many of whom had only been in the army six months, perished during their first night in the open.

The army dragged itself forward, littering the road with its dead, dying and deranged. We were constantly harassed by bands of Cossacks, greedy for booty, who threw themselves on stragglers or small detachments. In order to beat off such attacks, armed men gathered in bands and there were running battles in the snow with a few pieces of artillery, dragged all this way without horses, firing their final discharges in Russia.

Mixed in with such bravery was, however, as much cruelty and a revolting selfishness. The strongest pillaged the weakest, the sick were stripped of their clothing and the dying were robbed of their clothes and left to die in the deep snow. An instinct for self-preservation had snuffed out all traces of humanity in the human heart.

90
THE LICHTENSTEIN CAFÉ, 7 DECEMBER

We finally reached Vilna, which, like Smolensk before it, was the goal of all those who had survived the disaster to date. Vilna was inhabited, had well-stocked magazines, and could boast of food and other kinds of luxury – indeed, all the things we had done without since leaving Moscow. Each and every soldier had been borne along by the hope of reaching Vilna, but that hope was to be cruelly misplaced. Vilna was nothing more than the tomb of thousands, and those that survived were soon forced out, just as at Smolensk.

The most fortunate arrived before the bulk of the army reached the town. They found themselves quarters, food and other essentials. Some officers of the 25th Division were, luckily, numbered among this group, reached the town before the army and eagerly sought out the Lichtenstein Café. This establishment became our headquarters, and all surviving officers of the Division made their way there, even those who only made it on the 9th.

On the 9th the bulk of the army, some 40,000 desperate men, arrived before Vilna in a state of the most abject confusion. Pursued by Russian columns, they threw themselves into the town, although thousands were crushed to death at the gates. Just as at the Beresina, a crowd of deranged, desperate individuals, trampling the dying underfoot, stormed forward in an attempt to get into the safety of the town's streets. The frightened inhabitants bolted their doors and refused entry to anyone. It was a heart-rending sight to see the crowd of unfortunates, covered in rags, supplicating in the streets as the temperature dropped to 28 degrees. In vain did they seek shelter; even the magazines were closed to them as written permission was required to enter therein. Nor was there any room in the hospitals and barracks: these had long been filled to the brim, their long corridors and fireless rooms choked with the dead and dying and presenting a picture of utter horror.

The Jews behaved badly towards us. Whilst the Allied army had still been present in force, they came and offered their services and goods and even invited individuals into their houses. However, as soon as news of the Russian approach was received they threw Allied troops out into the cold streets, thereby seeking to ingratiate themselves in the eyes of the victors.

Amidst all the scenes of horror and destruction, the rumble of cannon was a timely reminder that we had to quit the town at once. The Russians were attacking our rearguard, and no sooner had we left from one side of the town, on the 10th, than the Cossacks entered the other. The Grande Armée resumed its march, heading towards Kovno.

91
NEAR EVE, 11 DECEMBER

We left Vilna on the 10th and abandoned thousands of dead, dying and prisoners. We managed to avoid the chaos at Ponari, which cost the army most of the rest of its artillery and transport – and even the Imperial Treasury – and made our weary way towards Kovno, protected by a weak rearguard but still suffering from the relentless cold. A vast number of men died on this final forced march.

We finally reached Eve, a small town familiar to us from having passed through it that very summer. How things had changed! Eve was stripped of the charms of summer, abandoned and partially buried under the deep snow. And the town, which in the summer had seen a brilliant army march through, was now obliged to see its ghostly streets play host to groups of miserable individuals, ruined by the Russian climate and by hunger and hoping for nothing more than to reach the banks of the Niemen at Kovno.

92
BETWEEN BRAUNSBERG AND ELBING, 21 DECEMBER

As 1812 came to an end, so too did the incredible suffering: the fatal retreat from Moscow was over. So too was the Grande Armée: it no longer existed. It left its glorious remains on the fields of Krasnoi, Smolensk, Valutina, Polotsk, Borodino and Malojaroslavets and over the endless steppes of Russia. It had been consumed by disease, hunger, want and the rigours of a wrathful climate.

Those that survived crossed the Niemen and made their way to various points along the Vistula. III Corps collected first at Danzig, then at Thorn and then at Inovratslav. The retreat therefore came to an end, as the troops went their different ways, marching off to their assigned places of rendezvous.

This plate shows a group of officers somewhere along the road between Braunsberg and Elbing. They have just had a brief meal before, once more, setting out and making their way to their overnight stop and welcome shelter.

III CORPS ON 25 JUNE 1812

Commanded by Marshal Michel Ney, Duc d'Elchingen
General of Brigade Gouré serving as Chief of Staff
General of Division Foucher serving as Corps Artillery Commander
Dr Jeantel serving as Principal Surgeon

10TH DIVISION (Ledru des Essarts)

1st Brigade (Gengoult)
24th Light (4 battalions) under Colonel Bellair
1st Regiment of the Portuguese Legion (2 battalions) under Colonel Pego

2nd Brigade (Marion)
46th Line (4 battalions) under Colonel Baudinot

3rd Brigade (Bruny)
72nd Line Regiment (4 battalions) under Colonel Lafitte
129th Line Regiment (Germans) (2 battalions) under Colonel Freytag

Divisonal artillery commanded by Captain Ragmey

11TH DIVISION (Razout)

1st Brigade (Joubert)
4th Line (4 battalions) under Colonel Massy
18th Line (4 battalions) under Colonel Pelleport

2nd Brigade (Compère)
2nd Regiment of the Portuguese Legion (2 battalions) under Colonel Javier
Illyrian Regiment (4 battalions) under Colonel Schmitz

3rd Brigade (d'Henin)
93rd Line Regiment (4 battalions) under Colonel Baudin

Divisional artillery commanded by Major Bernard

25TH DIVISION (Prince Royal of Württemberg, later General Marchand)
Prince's Staff: General of Brigade de Théobald, Major von Spitzemberg, Lt-Col D'Amerongen, Major von Wimpfen
Chief of Staff: General von Scheler, assisted by Captain Lesuire, General von Kerner, Colonel von Bangold, Colonel von Gelbke, Lieutenant von Miller, Lieutenant von Kampe and Adjutant Delagrange
Provost: Colonel von Nauseater
Gendarmes: 26 officers and men under Lieutenant Schiller
Administration: von Schoenlin, von Becker, Oetinger, Schlotterbeck and Krais
Protestant ministers: Hutten and Greber
Catholic priests: Pregler and Funck
Detached to Imperial Headquarters (IHQ): Colonel von Beroldingen, Captain Blücher, Lieutenant Livreville
Volunteers: Prince Adam and Major Wagner

1st Brigade (von Hügel, ADC Lieutenant von Reuss)
1st Württemberg (Prince Paul) Line (2 battalions) under Prince Paul Dernbach; 27 officers, 1,173 men

4th Württemberg Line (2 battalions) under Colonel von Roeder; 28 officers, 1,235 men

2nd Brigade (von Koch, ADC von Martens)
2nd Württemberg (Duke Wilhelm) Line (2 battalions) under Duke Wilhelm; 29 officers, 1,309 men
6th Württemberg (Crown Prince) Line (2 battalions); 27 officers, 1,220 men

3rd Brigade (von Bruselles, ADC von Dietrich)
3rd Light Infantry Battalion under Major Seeger; 15 officers, 668 men
4th Light Infantry Battalion under Major Scheidemantel; 14 officers, 670 men
1st Jäger Battalion König under Major Cornotte; 15 officers, 675 men
2nd Jäger Battalion under Major Stockmayer; 15 officers, 674 men

Divisional artillery commanded by Major von Brandt (ADC von Roeder):
1st and 2nd Horse Artillery Batteries; 6 officers, 250 men
1st and 2nd Foot Artillery Batteries (Lt-Col von Bartruff); 4 officers, 160 men
1 Reserve Battery; 2 officers, 171 men
Engineers (Colonel von Arlt)

III CORPS' CAVALRY (Wollrath)

9th Light Brigade (Mouriez)
11th Hussars (4 squadrons) under Colonel Collaert
6th Chevaulégers-lanciers Regiment (3 squadrons) under Colonel Marbeuf
4th Württemberg Jäger zu Pferd (König)

Regiment (4 squadrons) under Prince von Salm; 21 officers, 464 men

14th Light Brigade (Beurmann)
28th Chasseurs (2 squadrons) under Colonel La Roche
4th Chasseurs (4 squadrons) under Colonel Boulnois
1st Württemberg Chevaulégers (Prinz Adam) Regiment (4 squadrons) under Colonel von Brockfeld; 23 officers, 509 men
2nd Württemberg Chevaulégers (Leib) Regiment (4 squadrons) under Colonel von Normann; 22 officers, 496 men

Detached:
3rd Württemberg Jäger zu Pferd (Duke Louis) Regiment (4 squadrons) under Colonel Waldburg attached to III Cavalry Corps.
7th Württemberg Line (2 battalions) (in garrison at Danzig)

Corps Artillery Reserve
1st Foot Artillery
9th Foot Artillery

Corps Artillery Train
6th Train Battalion (5 companies)
14th Train Battalion (3 companies)
2nd Military Equipage Battalion (2 companies)
10th Ambulance Company
1st Pontoon Battalion (1 company)
1st Sapper Battalion (1 company)
3rd Sapper Battalion (2 companies)
Gendarmes (75 men)

BIBLIOGRAPHY
EYEWITNESS ACCOUNTS OF NAPOLEON'S INVASION OF RUSSIA

Napoleon's *Grande Armée*

Anon, *Erinnerungen eines Preussischen Offiziers aus den Jahren 1812 bis 1814*, Koblenz, 1846. (X Corps)

Anon, *Interessante Scenen aus den Feldzugen 1812 u. 1813*, in *Briefen eines deutschen Offizers*, Ludwigsburg, 1813.

Anon, 'Quelques notes par un capitaine au 16e de chasseurs à cheval qui fait la campagne', in G. Bertin's *La Campagne de 1812*, Paris, 1895. (16th Chasseurs, I Cavalry Corps)

Abbell, J., *L'odyssée d'un Carabinier à Cheval*, Brussels, 1969.

Adam, Albrecht, *Voyage de Willenberg en Prusse jusqu'à Moscou en 1812*, Munich, 1828. (Staff, IV Corps)

Ali, Mameluck, *Souvenirs du Mameluck Ali sur l'Empereur Napoléon*, Paris, 1926. (Mamelukes, Imperial Guard)

Aubry, Capitaine, *Souvenirs du 12ème de Chasseurs*, Paris, 1889. (12th Chasseurs, II Cavalry Corps)

Bacler d'Albe, Baron Louis-Albert-Guislain, *Souvenirs Pittoresques*, 2 vols, Paris 1898–92. (Topographical Department, IHQ)

Bangofsky, Georges, *Les étapes de G. Bangofsky, officier lorrain*, Paris, 1905. (Vilna Garrison)

Baumann, F., *Mit der großen Armee 1812 (Nach dem Bericht eines Mitkämpfers)*, Hamburg, 1910. (Westphalian Garde Chevaulégers, VIII Corps)

Bausset, Louis-François-Joseph, *Mémoires anecdotiques sur l'intérieur du Palais et sur quelques événements de l'Empire depuis 1805 jusqu'au 1 May 1814*, 4 vols, Paris, 1827–29. (Prefect of the Palace, IHQ)

Beauchamp, A. de, *Mémoires secrets et inédits pour servir à l'histoire contemporaine*, Paris, 1825. Includes Pierre-Louis Beavollier's *Mémoires sur l'expédition de Russie* and Jean Gazo's *Mémoires relatives à l'expédition de Russie.*

Begos, Louis, *Souvenirs de campagnes de lieutenant-général Louis Begos, ancien capitaine adjudant-major au 2e régiment suisse au service de la France*, Lausanne, 1859. (2nd Swiss Regiment, II Corps)

Berthezène, Général Pierre, *Souvenirs Militaires de la République et de l'Empire*, 2 vols, Paris, 1855.

Bertolini, Bartolomeo, *La Mia Prigionia*, Trieste, 1859. (Staff, IV Corps)

Bertrand, Vincent, *Mémoires du capitaine Vincent Bertrand*, Angers, 1909. (7th Light, I Corps)

Beulay, Honoré, *Mémoires d'un grenadier de la Grande Armée*, Paris, 1907. (36th Line, IX Corps)

Bial, Jean-Pierre, *Les Cahiers du Colonel Bial*, Brive, 1926.

Bialkowski, Antonin, *Pamietniki starego zolnierza, 1806–1814*, Warsaw, 1903.

Biot, Hubert-François, *Souvenirs anecdotiques et militaires du colonel Biot, aide de camp du général Pajol*, Paris, 1901. (ADC to General Pajol, I Corps' cavalry)

Blumröder, Graf von, *Meine Erlebnisse im Krieg und Frieden*, Sonderhausen, 1857.

Bomsdorf, Röder von, *Mittheilungen aus dem russischen Feldzuge*, Leipzig, 1816. (Prinz Albrecht Chevaulégers, III Cavalry Corps)

Bonneval, Général, Marquis de, *Mémoires anecdotiques*, Paris, 1900.

Borcke, Johann von, *Kriegerleben des Johann von Borcke, weiland kgl. preuss. Obersteleutnants, 1806–15*, Berlin, 1888. (ADC to General Ochs, 23rd Division, VIII Corps)

Boulart, Jean-François, *Mémoires Militaires du général Boulart sur les guerres de la République et de l'Empire*, Paris, 1892. (Artillery, Imperial Guard)

Bourgeois, René, *Tableau de la campagne de 1812, par Bourgeois témoin oculaire*, Paris, 1814.

Bourgogne, Adrien-Jean-Baptiste-François, *Mémoires publiés d'après le manuscrit original par Paul Cottin*, Paris, 1898. Translated as *The Memoirs of Sergeant Bourgogne, 1812–1813*, London, 1899. Reprinted London, 1979 and 1992. (Fusiliers-Grenadiers, Imperial Guard)

Bourgoing, Baron Paul-Charles-Amable de, *Souvenirs militaires du Baron de Bourgoing*, Paris, 1897. (5th Tirailleurs, Young Guard)

Brandt, Heinrich von, *Souvenirs d'un officier polonais*, Paris, 1879. Translated as *In the Legions of Napoleon*, London, 1999. (2nd Regiment of the Vistula Legion, Young Guard)

Bréaut des Marlots, Jean, *Lettre d'un capitaine de cuirassiers sur la campagne de Russie*, Paris, 1885. (Attached to IHQ)

Bro, Louis, *Mémoires du général Bro*, Paris, 1914. (Chasseurs à cheval, Imperial Guard)

Bucher, J. F., *Das Tagebuch einer Luzernerin aus dem Feldzuge nach Russland, 1812*, Lucerne, 1901.

Bussy, Marc, 'Notes de Jean-Marc Bussy', in Vol. V of *Soldats suisse au service étranger*, Geneva, 1913. (3rd Swiss Line, II Corps)

Buettner, Korporal, *Beschreibung der schicksale des ehmaligen Korporals Buettner wahr. sein. 19 montal. Gefangenschaft in Russland 1812/1813*, Nuremberg, 1831. (5th Bavarian Chevaulégers, attached to IV Corps)

Calosso, Jean, *Mémoires d'un vieux soldat*, Turin, 1857. (24th Chasseurs, II Corps)

Castellane, Victor, *Journal de maréchal de Castellane*, 5 vols. Paris, 1895–97. (IHQ)

Caulaincourt, Général Armande de, *Mémoires du général de Caulaincourt, duc de Vicenze*, 3 vols. Paris, 1933. Translated as (Vol. 1) *Memoirs of General de Caulaincourt*, London, 1935; and (Vol. 2) *No Peace with Napoleon*, London, 1936. (IHQ)

Chapuis, Colonel M., *Campagne de 1812 en Russie*, Paris, 1856. (85th Line Regiment, I Corps)

Chevalier, Jean-Michel, *Souvenirs des guerres napoléoniennes*, Paris, 1970. (Chasseurs à Cheval, Imperial Guard)

Chlapowski, Désiré, *Mémoires sur les guerres de Napoléon, 1806–1813*, Paris, 1908. Translated as *Memoirs of a Polish Lancer*, Chicago, 1992. (Polish Lancers, Imperial Guard)

Coignet, Jean-Roch, *Cahiers*, Paris, 1883. Translated as *The Note-Books of Captain Coignet*, London, 1928. Reprinted 1986 and 1998. (2nd Grenadiers à Pied, Imperial Guard)

Combes, Colonel, *Mémoires sur les campagnes de Russie, de Saxe et de France*, Paris, 1896. (8th Chasseurs, III Cavalry Corps)

Comeau, Sebastian-Joseph de, *Souvenirs des guerres d'Allemagne pendant la Révolution et l'Empire*, Paris, 1900. (Chief of Staff, 20th Division, VI Corps)

Constantin, Pierre de, *Un Cavalier de la Grande Armée*, Paris, 1925. (IHQ)

Coudreux, Alexandre, *Lettres du commandant Coudreux à son frère*, Paris, 1908. (15th Light, I Corps)

Curely, Jean Nicolas, *Le général Curely. Itinéraire d'un cavalier léger de la Grande Armée*, Paris, 1887. (20th Chasseurs, II Corps)

Déchy, Edouard, *Souvenirs d'un garde du corps du roi de la compagnie de Noailles, suivis de souvenirs d'Allemagne et de Russie*, Paris, 1869.

Dellard, Baron Jean Pierre, *Mémoires Militaires du général Baron Dellard*, Paris, 1892.

Dedem van der Gelder, Baron de, *Mémoires du général baron de Dedem de Gelder*, Plon-Nourrit, Paris, 1900. (Commanded 2nd Brigade, 2nd Division, I Corps)

Dembinski, Henryk, *Pamietnik Henryka Dembinskiego Jeneraa Wojsk Polskich*, Poznan, 1860.

Demonts, Bernard, *La carrière militaire du général Demonts, sous le Consulat et l'Empire*, Auch, 1925.

Dode de la Brunerie, Guillaume, *Episode de la guerre de 1812*, Grenoble, 1873.

Drujon de Beaulieu, Comte de, *Souvenirs d'un militaire pendant quelques années du regne de Napoléon*, Belley, 1831. (8th Chevau-légers, II Corps)

Ducor, Henri, *Aventures d'un marin de la Garde Impériale, prisonnier de guerre sur les pontons espagnols, dans les îles de Cabrera et en Russie*, 2 vols, Paris, 1833. (Sailors, Imperial Guard)

Dumas, Mathieu, *Souvenirs de Lieutenant-Général Comte Mathieu Dumas, de 1770 à 1836*, 3 vols, Paris, 1839. (Intendant General, IHQ)

Dumonceau, François, *Mémoires du Général Comte François Dumonceau*, 3 vols, Brussels, 1958–63. (Dutch Lancers, Imperial Guard)

Dupuy, Victor, *Souvenirs Militaires, 1794–1816*, Paris, 1892. (2nd Chasseurs, I Corps' cavalry)

Dutheillet de la Mothe, Aubin, *Mémoires du Lieutenant-Colonel Aubin Dutheillet de la Mothe*, Brussels, 1899. (57th Line, I Corps)

Duverger, P.T., *Mes aventures dans la campagne de Russie*, Paris, 1833. (Surgeon, I Cavalry Corps)

Eniden, Fritz, *Erinnerungen eines österreichischen Ordonnanzoffiziers aus dem Feldzuge 1812*, Vienna, 1898. (Austrian Corps)

Faber du Faur, G. de, *La campagne de Russie d'après le journal illustré d'un témoin oculaire*, Paris, 1895. (Württemberg artillery, III Corps)

Fain, Baron Agathon Jean François, *Manuscrit de 1812*, Leipzig, 1827. (IHQ)

Fantin des Odoards, Louis Florimond, *Journal du général Fantin des Odoards*, Paris, 1895. (1st Grenadiers à Pied, Imperial Guard)

Faré, Charles-Armand, *Lettres d'une jeune officier à sa mère, 1803–1814*, Paris, 1863. (Grenadiers, Imperial Guard)

Faure, Raymond, *Souvenirs du nord, ou la guerre, la Russie et les Russes ou l'esclavage*, Paris, 1821. (I Cavalry Corps)

Fézensac, M. le Duc de, *Souvenirs militaires de 1804 à 1814*, Paris, 1863. Translated and abridged as *A Journal of the Russian Campaigns of 1812*, London, 1852. (4th Line, III Corps)

Fleck, *Beschreibung meiner Leiden und schicksale während Napoleons Feldzuege und meiner Gefangenschaft in Russland*, Hildesheim, 1845. (Westphalian Guard Jägers, VIII Corps)

Franchi, Lieutenant, *Récit de Franchi, sous-officier dans la compagnie d'élite des 8ème Chasseurs à cheval*, Le Mans, 1861. (8th Chasseurs, III Cavalry Corps)

François, Charles, *Journal du Capitaine François, 1793–1830*, 2 vols. Paris, 1903–4. Translated as *From Valmy to Waterloo*, London, 1906. (30th Line, I Corps)

Fredro, Aleksandr, *Trzy po Trzy: Pamietniki z Epoki Napoleonskiej*, Warsaw, 1917. Published in French as *Sans Queue ni Tête: Mémoires*, Paris, 1992.

Freytag, Jean-David, *Mémoires du général Freytag*, 2 vols, Paris, 1824. (Commanded 3rd Brigade, 10th Division, III Corps, from November 1812)

Funck, F. von, *In Russland und Sachsen, 1812–1815*, Dresden, 1930. Translated as *In the Wake of Napoleon: Being the Memoirs of Ferdinand von Funck, Lieutenant General in the Saxon Army and Adjutant to the King of Saxony*, London, 1931. (Commanded 22nd Division, VII Corps)

Furtenbach, K. von, *Krieg gegen Russland und russische Gefangenschaft*, Leipzig, 1912. (VI Corps)

Gardier, Louis, *Journal de la campagne de Russie en 1812*, Paris, 1999. (3rd Line, XI Corps)

Gajewski, Franciszek, *Pamietniki Franciszka Gajewskiego, Pulkownika Wojsk Polskich*, 2 vols, Poznan, 1913.

Gelderblom, *Wehrstand und Lehrstand – Erinnerungen aus den Feldzügen nach Russland und Frankreich*, Elberfeld, 1847.

Gervais, Capitaine, *A la conquête de l'Europe: Souvenirs d'un soldat de la Révolution et de l'Empire*, Paris, 1939.

Giesse, Friedrich, *Kassel–Moskau–Kuestrin: Tagebuch während des russischen Feldzugs geführt*, Leipzig, 1912. (5th Westphalian Line, VIII Corps)

Girod de l'Ain, Général Baron, *Dix ans de mes souvenirs militaires (1805–1815)*, Paris, 1873.

Goethe, *Aus dem leben eines sächsischen Husaren*, Leipzig, 1853. (Saxon Hussars, VII Corps)

Grabowski, Josef, *Mémoires Militaires*, Paris, 1907. (Polish Lancers, Imperial Guard)

Griois, Lubin, *Mémoires du général Griois, 1792–1822*, 2 vols, Paris, 1909. (Commanded artillery, III Cavalry Corps)

Grüber, Carl Johann Ritter von, *Souvenirs du chevalier Grüber*, Paris, 1909. (Austrian Corps)

Guerre, Michel, *Mémoires de Michel Guerre*, Agen, 1928.

Guibert, Florent, *Souvenirs d'un sous-lieutenant d'infanterie légère*, Paris, 1997. (26th Light, II Corps)

Guillemard, Robert, *Adventures of a French Sergeant during his Campaigns in Italy, Spain, Germany,*

Russia, from 1805 to 1823, London, 1826. (IV Corps)

Guitard, Joseph, *Souvenirs militaires du Premier Empire: Mémoires d'un grenadier de la Garde*, Paris, 1934. (2nd Grenadiers à Pied, Imperial Guard)

Hausmann, Franz, *A Soldier for Napoleon: The Campaigns of Lieutenant Franz Joseph Hausmann, 7th Bavarian Infantry*, London, 1998. (7th Bavarian Infantry, VI Corps)

Henckens, Lieutenant J. L., *Mémoires se rapportant à son service militaire au 6ème Régiment de Chasseurs à cheval français de 1803 à 1816*, The Hague, 1910. (6th Chasseurs, III Cavalry Corps)

Hochberg, Wilhelm, Graf von, *La campagne de 1812: Mémoires du Margrave de Bade*, Paris, 1912. (Commanded 3rd Brigade, 26th Division, IX Corps)

Hogendorp, Dirk van, *Mémoires du général Dirk van Hogendorp, comte de l'Empire*, The Hague, 1887. (Governor of Lithuania)

Jourdain, Armand, *Trente-neuf jours de réclusion dans les prisons de Vilna en 1812*, Bayeux, 1858. (Surgeon)

Kampfen, A., *Deux cahiers des souvenirs*, Neufchatel, 1962.

Kergorre, Alexandre Bellot de, *Une commissaire de guerres pendant le premier empire*, Paris, 1899. (Commissary Officer, IHQ)

Kirchoff, J. de, *Observations médicales faites pendant les campagnes de Russie en 1812 et en Allemagne en 1813*, Maestricht, 1814.

Klinkhardt, J., *Feldzugs-erinnerungen aus den Jahren 1812–1815*, Braunschweig, 1908. (Westphalian)

Koenig, W. von, *Bericht über seine Teilnahme am russischen Feldzug*, Stuttgart, 1987. (1st Württemberg Chasseurs, III Corps)

Kozmian, Kajetan, *Pamietniki Kajetana Kozmiana Obejmujace Wspomnienia od Roku 1780–1815*, 3 vols, Poznan, 1858–65.

Kurz, Hauptmann von, *Der Feldzug von 1812: Denkwüdigkeiten eines württembergischen offiziers*, Esslingen, 1838. (4th Württemberg Line, III Corps)

Labaume, Eugène, *Rélation circonstanciée de la campagne de Russie*, Paris, 1814. Translated as *A Circumstantial Narrative of the Campaign in Russia*, London, 1814. (Staff, IV Corps)

Lagneau, Louis, Comte de, *Journal d'un chirurgien de la Grande Armée, 1803–1815*, Paris, 1913. (Surgeon to Fusiliers-Grenadiers, Imperial Guard)

Larrey, Dominique, *Mémoires de chirurgie militaire et campagnes*, Paris, 1812–17. (Surgeon, IHQ)

Laugier, Césare de, *Gl'italiani in Russia per servire alla storia della Russia, della Polonia e dell'Italia nel 1812*, 4 vols, Milan, 1826–7. (Guards of Honour, Italian Royal Guard, IV Corps)

Lebardier, *Notes sur la campagne de Russie en 1812,*

par un officier de la Grande Armée, Paris, 1908.

Legler, Thomas, *Denkwüdigkeiten aus dem Russischen Feldzuge vom Jahre 1812*, Bern, 1942. (1st Swiss Line, II Corps)

Leissnig, W. L., *Märshe und krieger lebnisse in Jahre 1812*, Budissia, 1828. (Saxon Chevau-légers Prinz Albrecht, II Cavalry Corps)

Lejeune, Baron Louis François, *Mémoires du général Lejeune*, 2 vols, Paris, Firmin-Didot, 1896. Translated as *The Memoirs of Baron Lejeune*, London, 1897. (ADC to Marshal Berthier, IHQ)

Lemoine-Montigny, E., *Souvenirs anecdotiques d'un officier de la Grande Armée*, Paris, 1833.

Leroy, Claude F. M., *Souvenirs de Leroy, major d'infanterie*, Dijon, 1908. (85th Line, I Corps)

Levavasseur, Octave. R. F., *Souvenirs Militaires d'Octave Levavasseur, officier d'artillerie*, Paris, 1914. (Artillery, Imperial Guard)

Lignières, Marie-Henri, Comte de, *Souvenirs de la Grande Armée et de la Vieille Garde Impériale*, Paris, 1933. (1st Chasseurs à Pied, Imperial Guard)

Limon, Constant de, 'Lettres de Constant de Limon', in appendices of *Mémoires de Felix de Limon*, Brussels, 1949. (1st Chasseurs, I Corps)

Lindemann, F., *Meine Gefangenschaft in Russland, 1812–13*, Ronneburg, 1833.

Lorencz, Guillaume Latrille de, *Souvenirs militaires du général comte de Lorencz*, Paris, 1902. (Staff, II Corps)

Lossberg, Friedrich Wilhelm von, *Briefe in der Heimat geschrieben während des Feldzuges 1812 in Russland*, Kassel, 1844. (3rd Westphalian Line, VIII Corps)

MacDonald, Marshal, *Souvenirs de maréchal MacDonald, duc de Tarante*, Paris, 1905. (Commanded X Corps)

Maillard, Jean Pierre, 'Mémoires de Jean-Pierre Maillard de Vevey', in *Soldats Suisses au service étranger*, Geneva, 1913.

Mailly-Nesle, Adrien Augustin Amalric, *Mon journal pendant la campagne de Russie écrit du mémoire après mon retour à Paris*, Paris, 1841. (2nd Carabiniers, II Cavalry Corps)

Mändler, *Erinnerungen aus meinen Feldzügen*, Nürnberg, 1854. (Bavaria, VI Corps)

Marbot, Antoine-Marcellin, *Mémoires du général Baron de Marbot*, 3 vols, Paris, 1891. Translated as *The Memoirs of Baron de Marbot*, 2 vols, London, 1892 and 1988. (23rd Chasseurs, II Corps)

Maret, Hugues Bernard, Duc de Bassano, *Souvenirs intimes de la Révolution et de l'Empire*, 2 vols, Brussels, 1843. (Foreign Minister, based at Vilna)

Marsac, Sergent, *La Bérésina – Souvenirs d'un soldat de la Grande Armée*, Limoges, n.d.

Martens, Christian Septimus von, *Vor fünfzig Jahre: Tagebuch meines Feldzuges in Russland, 1812*, Stuttgart, 1862. (6th Württemberg Line, III Corps)

Materre, Général, *Général Materre, d'après ses souvenirs militaires inédits*, Paris, 1906.

Mayer, Pierre-Louis, 'Mémoires inédits d'un prisonnier en Russie', in *Soldats Suisses au service étranger*, Geneva, 1908. (2nd Swiss Line, II Corps)

Meerheimb, Franz Ludwig August von, *Erlebnisse eines Veteranen der grossen Armee während des Feldzuges in Russland, 1812*, Dresden, 1860. (Saxon Guard Cuirassiers)

Meier, *Erinnerungen aus den Feldzugen, 1806–1815*, Karlsruhe, 1854. (Baden, IX Corps)

Merme, Jean-Marie, *Des Pyramides à Moscou: Souvenirs d'un soldat de Napoléon Premier*, Paris, 1852. (Chasseurs à Cheval, Imperial Guard)

Mercx de Corbais, Eduard de, *Le général major baron Eduard de Mercx de Corbais, notice biographique par R. Marchot (sometimes referred to as being by Warchot)*, Namur, 1855. (8th Chevau-légers, II Corps)

Mesnage de Gagny, Louis de, *Ma malheureuse campagne de Russie, 1812–14*, Caen, 1910. (Partonneux's division, IX Corps)

Montesquiou, Anatole, Comte de, *Souvenirs sur la Révolution, l'Empire, la Restauration et le règne de Louis-Philippe*, Paris, 1961.

Montravel, A. de, *Voyage d'un officier prisonnier en Russie*, Paris, 1817. (25th Line, I Corps)

Moricheau-Beaupré, Dr, *Effets et propriétés du froid, avec un aperçu historique et médical sur la campagne de Russie*, Montpellier, 1817.

Muraldt, Albrecht von, *Beresina*, Bern, 1942. (5th Bavarian Chevau-légers, attached to IV Corps)

Nieritz, Colonel, *Abenderzahlungen von seiner Kriegsthaten unter Napoleon gegen Russland, 1812*, Neuruppin, 1848.

Noël, Jean Nicholas August, *Souvenirs d'un officier du Premier Empire, 1795–1832*, Paris, 1895.

Oginski, Michel, *Mémoires de Michel Oginski sur la Pologne et les Polonaises*, 3 vols, Paris, 1827.

Oudinot, Marshal, *Le maréchal Oudinot, duc de Reggio, d'après les souvenirs inédits de la maréchale, par Gaston Steigler*, Paris, 1905. Translated as *Memoirs of Marshal Oudinot compiled from the hitherto unpublished souvenirs of the Duchesse de Reggio*, London, 1896. (Commanded II Corps)

Pagan, M., *Mémoires d'un prisonnier en Russie*, Lyon, 1843.

Paixhans, Général Henri Joseph de, *Retraite de Moscou*, Metz, 1868.

Pelet, Jean-Jacques-Germain, Baron, 'Bataille de la Moskowa', in vol. 7 of *Bibliothèque historique et militaire*, Paris, 1853.

Pelleport, Pierre, Vicomte de, *Souvenirs militaires et intimes du général vicomte de Pelleport de 1793 à 1853*, 2 vols, Paris, 1857. (18th Line, III Corps.

Peppler, F., *Schilderung meiner Gefangenschaft in*

Russland, 1812–14, Darmstadt, 1832. (Hessian Leibregiment, IHQ escort)

Persat, Maurice, *Mémoires du commandant Persat, 1806–1844*, Paris, 1910.

Peyrusse, Guillaume, *Lettres inédites du Baron Guillaume Peyrusse, écrites à son frère André pendant les campagnes de l'Empire de 1809 à 1814*, Paris, 1894. (Paymaster, Imperial Treasury)

Pfeister, *Aus dem Lager des Rheinbundes 1812 und 1813*, Stuttgart und Leipzig, 1897. (Württemberg)

Pils, François, *Journal de marche du Grenadier Pils, 1804–1814*, Paris, 1895. (Marshal Oudinot's servant, II Corps)

Pion des Loches, Antoine Augustin, *Mes Campagnes, 1792–1815: Notes et correspondence du colonel d'artillerie Pion des Loches*, Paris, 1889. (Artillery, Imperial Guard)

Planat de la Faye, Nicholas Louis, *Vie de Planat de la Faye, aide-de-camp des généraux Lariboisière et Drouet, officier d'ordonnance de Napoléon*, Paris, 1895. (Staff, Artillery Reserve)

Pontier, Raymond, *Souvenirs de chirurgien Pontier sur la retraite de Russie*, Brive, 1967.

Pouget, François René, *Souvenirs de guerre du général baron Pouget*, Paris, 1895. (Commanded 2nd Brigade of 8th Division, II Corps)

Pryzybylski, Zbigniew, *Military Memoirs of Zbigniew Pryzybylski*, Warsaw, n.d.

Putigny, Jean-Marie, *Putigny: Grognard de l'Empire*, Paris, 1950.

Puybusque, Louis Guillaume, *Lettres sur la guerre de Russie en 1812*, Paris, 1817. (Intendant officer, Smolensk)

Quaij, Charles de, *Charles de Quaij, capitaine de grenadiers de la Garde Imperiale sous Napoléon I*, Ruremonde, 1900.

Rapp, Jean, *Mémoires écrits par lui-même et publiés par sa famille*, Paris, 1823. Translated as *The Memoirs of General Count Rapp*, London, 1823, and Cambridge, 1985. (ADC to Napoleon, IHQ)

Raven, O. G. E., *Tagebuch des Feldzuges in Russland im Jahre 1812*, Berlin, n.d. (Mecklenburg-Schwerin)

Réguinot, Sergent, *Le soldat isolé: Histoire d'un soldat pendant la campagne de Russie*, Paris, 1831. (26th Light, II Corps)

Ricome, J. B., *Journal d'un grognard de l'Empire*, Paris, 1988.

Rigau, Diedonné, *Souvenirs des guerres de l'Empire, avec réflexions*, Paris, 1845. (Berthier's staff, IHQ)

Roch-Godart, Général, *Mémoires du général-baron Roch-Godart, 1792–1815*, Paris, 1895. (Governor of Vilna)

Röder, Franz, *Der Kriegszug Napoleons gegen Russland im Jahre 1812*, Leipzig, 1848. Translated (and edited by Helen Roeder) as *The Ordeal of Captain Roeder, from the Diary of an Officer of the First*

Battalion of Hessian Lifeguards during the Moscow Campaign of 1812–13, London, 1960.

Roguet, François. *Mémoires militaires du lieutenant-général comte Roguet, colonel en seconde des grenadiers à pied de la Vieille Garde*, 4 vols, Paris, 1862–65. (Commanded 2nd Division, Imperial Guard)

Roos, Heinrich von, *Ein Jahr aus meinem leben oder reise von den westlichen Ufern der Donau an die Nara, südlich von Moskva, und zurück an die Beresina, mit der grossen Armee Napoleons, im Jahre 1812*, St Petersburg, 1832. (3rd Württemberg Chasseurs, II Cavalry Corps)

Rosselet, Abraham, *Souvenirs de Abraham Rosselet, lieutenant-colonel en retraite au service de la France*, Neuchatel, 1857. (3rd Swiss Line, II Corps)

Rotenhan, Freiherr von, *Denkwürdigkeiten eines württembergischen Offiziers aus den Feldzuge im Jahre 1812*, Berlin, 1892.

Roustam, Raza, *Souvenirs de Roustam, mameluck de Napoléon*, Paris, 1821. (Mamelukes, IHQ)

Rumigny, Comte de, *Mémoires du général comte de Rumigny*, Paris, 1921.

Sachs, Karl, *Erinnerungs-Blatter eines Badischen soldaten an den Russischen feldzug von 1812 bis 1813*, Ulm, 1991. (IX Corps)

Saint-Chamans, Alfred Armand Robert, *Mémoires du général comte de Saint-Chamans, ancien aide-de-camp du Maréchal Soult*, Paris, 1896. (7th Chasseurs, II Corps)

St-Cyr, Laurent Gouvion, *Mémoires pour servir à l'histoire militaire sous le directoire, le consulat et l'Empire*, Paris, 1831. (Commanded VI Corps)

Sauvage, N. J., *Rélation de la Campagne de Russie*, Paris, 1827.

Sayve, A. de, *Souvenirs de Pologne et scènes militaires du campagne de Russie, 1812*, Paris, 1833. (Cuirassiers)

Schauroth, Graf von, *Im Rheinbund-Regiment der Herzoglich Sächsischen Kontingente während der Feldzüge in Tirol, Spanien und Russland*, Berlin, 1905 (XI Corps)

Schel, C., *Vom Rhein zur Moskwa, 1812*, Krefeld, 1957. (2nd Carabineer Regiment, II Cavalry Corps)

Scheltens, *Souvenirs d'un vieux soldat belge de la garde impériale*, Brussels, 1880. (2nd Grenadiers à Pied, Imperial Guard)

Schrafel, Joseph, *Merkwürdige Schicksale des ehemaligen Feldwebels im kongl. bayer. 5te Linien-Infanterie-Regiment, Joseph Schrafel, vorzüglich im russischen Feldzuge und in der Gefangenschaft, in den Jahren 1812 bis 1814, von ihm selbstbeschrieben*, Nuremberg, 1834. (5th Bavarian Line, VI Corps)

Schumacher, Gaspard, *Journal et Souvenirs, 1798–1830*, Paris, 1900. (Swiss)

Ségur, Phillipe, Comte de, *Du Rhin à Fontainebleau:*

Mémoires du général comte de Ségur, Paris, 1910. (Assistant Prefect of the Palace, IHQ)

Sérang, Marquis de, *Les prisonniers français en Russie: Mémoires et souvenirs de M. le marquis de Sérang, recueillis et publiés par M. de Puybusque*, 2 vols, Paris, 1837.

Séruzier, Théodore Jean Joseph, Baron, *Mémoires militaires du baron Séruzier, colonel d'artillerie légère*, Paris, 1824. (Artillery, II Cavalry Corps)

Soden, Franz von, *Beitrage zur Gescheite des Krieges in den Jahren 1812 und 1813*, Arnstadt, 1821. (Saxon Duchies, XI Corps)

Solignac, A. de, *La Berezina: Souvenirs d'un soldat de la Grande Armée*, Isle, 1890.

Soltyk, Comte Roman, *Napoléon en 1812. Mémoires historiques et militaires sur la campagne de Russie*, Paris, 1836. (Topographical Department, IHQ)

Steinmüller, *Tagebuch über seine Teilnahme am russischen Feldzug 1812*, Heidelberg, 1903. (IX Corps)

Stendhal, M. de, *Journal de Stendhal*, Paris, 1888. (Commissary officer)

Suckow, Karl von, *Aus meinem Soldatenleben*, Stuttgart, 1862.

Surugué, Andrien, *Un Témoin de la campagne de Russie*, Paris, 1914.

Szymanowski, General Josef, *Mémoires du général Szymanowski*, Paris, Charles-Lavauzelle, 1900. (Polish Lancers, Imperial Guard)

Tascher, Maurice de, *Notes de campagne (1806–1813)*, Châteauroux, 1938. (Staff, IV Corps)

Taxis, A. von Thurn und, *Aus drei Feldzügen 1812 bis 1815: Erinnerungen des Prinzen August von Thurn und Taxis*, Leipzig, 1912. (ADC to General Wrede, VI Corps)

Theuss, *Rückblicke und Erinnerungen aus den Tagen meiner russischen Gefangenschaft*, Leipzig, 1816. (Saxon Duchies, XI Corps)

Thirion, Auguste de, *Souvenirs militaires, 1807–1818*, Paris, 1892. (2nd Cuirassiers, I Cavalry Corps)

Thomas, Prosper, *Souvenirs de Russie*, Epinal, 1844.

Trefcon, J., *Carnet de campagne*, Paris, 1914.

Vaudoncourt, Frédéric Guillaume de, *Critical Situation of Bonaparte in his Retreat out of Russia, by an Eye-witness*, London, 1815. (Commanded 2nd Brigade, 15th Division, IV Corps)

Victor, Claude Perrin, Marshal, Duc de Bellune, *Mémoires*, Paris, 1847. (Commanded IX Corps; Vols V and VI refer to Russia)

Vieillot, Rodolphe, *Souvenirs d'un prisonnier en Russie*, Paris, 1996.

Villiers, C. G. L., *Douze ans de campagnes*, Paris, n.d.

Vionnet, Louis-Joséph, *Campagnes de Russie et de Saxe, 1812–13*, Paris, 1899. (Fusiliers-Grenadiers, Imperial Guard)

Vossen, *Tagebuch*, Düsseldorf, 1891.

Vossler, Heinrich August, *With Napoleon in Russia:*

The Diary of a Lieutenant of the Grand Army, 1812–13, London, 1969. (3rd Württemberg Chasseurs, II Cavalry Corps)

Wachsmuth, J., *Geschichte meiner Kriegsgefangenschaft in Russland in den Jahren 1812 und 1813*, Magdeburg, 1910. (VIII Corps)

Walter, Jakob, *A Conscript in the Army of Napoleon*, New York, 1938. Reprinted in 1991 as *The Diary of a Napoleonic Foot Soldier*. (4th Württemberg Line, III Corps)

Wagvier, C. J., *Aanteekeningen gehouden gedurende mijnen marsch naar, gevangenschap in en torugreize uit Russland in 1812, 1813 e 1814*, Amsterdam, 1820.

Wautier, Baron, *Mémoires d'un officier Belge*, Paris, 2000. (VIII Corps)

Wedel, Carl Anton Wilhelm, Graf von, *Geschichte eines Offiziers im Kriege gegen Russland, 1812, in russischer Gefangenschaft 1813 bis 1814, im Feldzuge gegen Napoleon 1815, Lebenserinnerungen*, Berlin, 1897. (9th Chevau-légers, I Corps)

Wesemann, J. H. C., *Kanonier des Kaisers: Kriegstagenbuch der Heinrich Wesemann, 1808–14*, Cologne, 1971.

Zimmerman, Godfrey, *Autobiography of Godfrey Zimmerman, formerly in the Commissariat Department of the Army under Napoleon*, London, 1852.

Journals

Anon, 'Wspomnienia ulana pulku pierwszego legii nadwislanskiej o kampaniach lat 1807–1814', *Biblioteka Warszawska*, 1908.

Auvray, Pierre, 'Souvenirs militaires de Pierre Auvray, sous-lieutenant au 23ème régiment de dragons (1797–1815)', *Carnet de la Sabretache*, 1919. (23rd Dragoons, III Cavalry Corps)

Bailly, François-Joseph, 'Souvenirs et anecdotes de Joseph Bailly', *Revue des Etudes Historiques*, 1904.

Barrau, Jean-Pierre-Armand, 'Mémoires sur la campagne de Russie de 1812', *Rivista Italiana di Studi Napoleonici*, 1979. (Neapolitan Guard)

Bénard, Charles, 'Souvenirs de 1812: Un prisonnier français en Russie', *La Giberne*, 1904–07. (4th Line, III Corps)

Bismarck, Frederick von, 'Campagne de 1812', *Le Spectateur Militaire*, 1847. (3rd Wurttemberg Chasseurs, III Cavalry Corps)

Bonnet, Guillaume, 'Journal de Capitaine Bonnet du 18ème ligne', *Carnet de la Sabretache*, 1912. (18th Line, III Corps.)

Burnand, A., 'Mort d'un officier vaudois à la Bérésina', *Revue Historique Vaudoise*, 1908.

Chéron, Alexandre de, 'Mémoires inédits d'Alexandre de Chéron sur la campagne de Russie', *Revue de l'Institut Napoléon*, 1983.

Clemenso, H., 'Souvenirs d'un officier valaisan', *Annales Valaisannes*, 1957. (11th Light, II Corps)

Corbineau, Jean-Baptiste Juvenal Comte, 'Passage de la Bérésina', *Le Spectateur Militaire*, 1827. (Commanded 6th Light Cavalry Brigade, II Corps' cavalry)

Dandel, Lieutenant, 'Souvenirs de campagne du Lt Daniel du 9e Hussards', *Carnet de la Sabretache*, 1952. (9th Hussars, II Cavalry Corps)

Dornheim, 'Skizzen aus den Feldzügen des Batallions Lippe', *Lippisches Magazin*, 2, 1837. (XI Corps)

Everts, Henri-Pierre, 'Campagne et captivité en Russie', *Carnet de la Sabretache*, 1901. (33rd Light, I Corps)

Genty, M., 'Avec Napoléon en Russie', *Esculape*, 1913 (Surgeon, Württemberg Division, III Corps)

Guiraud, Alexandre, 'Journal de ma Vie', *Revue des Deux Mondes*, 1967–68. (Engineers, Imperial Guard)

Jacob, Paul-Irénée, 'Journal et itinéraire de dix ans de campagne (1800–1814)', *Revue d'Histoire de la Pharmacie*, 1966. (5th Artillery Regiment)

Jacquemont, Porphyre, 'Carnet de route d'un officier d'artillerie', *Souvenirs et Mémoires*, 1899. (5th Artillery Regiment)

Jolly, Colonel, 'Souvenirs et récits du colonel Jolly sur la campagne de Moscou', *Revue Hebdomadaire*, 1909.

Kalkreuth, Lieutenant von, 'Erinnerungen', *Zeitschrift fur kunst, wissenschaft und Geschichte des Krieges*, Vol V, 1835. (2nd Prussian Hussars, I Cavalry Corps)

La Flize, 'Souvenirs de la Moskowa par un chirurgien de la Garde Imperiale', *Feuilles d'Histoire*, 1912. (Surgeon, Imperial Guard)

Lassus-Marcilly, F. N., 'Notes sur la campagne de Russie', *Carnet de la Sabretache*, 1914. (2nd Artillery Regiment)

Lecoq, 'Journal d'un grenadier de la Garde', *Revue de Paris*, 1911. (Grenadiers à Cheval, Imperial Guard)

Lyautey, Hubert, 'Lettres d'un lieutenant de la Grande Armée', *La Revue des Deux Mondes*, December 1962. (Artillery, Imperial Guard)

Majou, L. J. L., 'Journal du commandant Majou', *Revue des Etudes Historiques*, 1899.

Maillinger, Joseph, 'Tagebuch des Hauptmanns Joseph Maillinger im Feldzuge nach Russland, 1812', *Darstellungen aus der Bayerischen Krieges- und Heeresgeschichte*, 1921.

Minod, Charles-François, 'Journal de mes campagnes et blessures', *Carnet de la Sabretache*, 1908. (2nd Swiss Line, II Corps)

Nottat, Nicolas, 'Souvenirs de la campagne de Russie', *Revue du Train*, 1953.

Pastoret, Amédée, 'De Witebsk à la Bérésina', *Revue de Paris*, April 1902. (Intendant, Byelorussia)

Pelet, Jean-Jacques-Germain, Baron, 'Carnets sur la campagne de Russie de 1812', *Carnet de la Sabretache*, 1906.

Poncelet, 'Souvenirs sur la campagne de Russie', *Revue Napoléonienne*, 1903–04.

Prétét, C. J., 'Rélation de la campagne de Russie', *Revue Bourguignonne*, 1893. (93rd Line, III Corps)

Preysing-Moos, Maximilian Graf von, 'Tagebuch des Generalmajors Maximilian Graf von Preysing-Moos, Führer der Bayerischen Kavallerie-Division im Feldzuge nach Russland, 1812', *Darstellungen aus der Bayerischen Krieges- und Heeresgeschichte*, 1912. (Commanded Bavarian cavalry, attached to IV Corps)

Rattier, Jean Henri, 'Notes d'un sergent-major', *Revue Rétrospective*, 1894.

Roederer, Pierre Louis, 'Notes d'un prisonnier en Russie', *Revue de Paris*, 1913. (8th Chevau-légers, II Corps.)

Rossetti, Marie-Joséph-Thomas, 'Journal inédit', *Revue de France*, 1931–32. (ADC to Murat, Commander of Reserve Cavalry)

Sarrant, Pierre, 'Premier Empire: Les souvenirs de Pierre Sarrant, chirurgien aux armées impériales', *Bulletin de la Société Scientifique, Historique et Archéologique de la Correze*, 1972.

Suhay, Imre, 'Egy magyar huszartiszt feljegyzesei I' (The Notes of a Hungarian Hussar Officer in Napoleon I's Campaign in Russia), *Hadtortenelmi Kozlemenyek*, 1941. (Austrian Corps)

Teste, François Anton, 'Souvenirs du général baron Teste', *Carnet de la Sabretache*, 1906–07 and 1911–12. (Commanded 2nd Brigade, 5th Division, I Corps)

Thévenin, Maurice, 'Mémoires d'un vieux de la vieille', *Bulletin de la Société des Sciences Historiques et Naturelles de l'Yonne*, 1959–60. (17th Line, I Corps)

Turno, Charles, 'Souvenirs d'un officier polonais', *Revue des Etudes Napoléoniennes*, 33, 1931. (ADC to General Turno, IV Cavalry Corps)

Venturini, Joseph, 'Carnets d'un Italien au service de France', *Nouvelle Revue Rétrospective*, 1904.

Vilde, Jean Marie Pierre Aubry de, 'Lettres d'un officier pendant la campagne de Russie', *Revue des Etudes Historiques*, 1922.

Viot, Capitaine, 'Le général Pajol en 1812', *Carnet Historique et Littéraire*, 1899. (ADC to Pajol, I Corps)

Zalusky, Joseph-Henri, 'Souvenirs du général comte Zalusky', *Carnet de la Sabretache*, 1897. (Polish Lancers, Imperial Guard)

Russian

Anon, *Lettres d'un vétéran de l'armée russe en 1812*.

Anon, *Sketch of a Journal of the Retreat and Flight of the French Armies from Moscow. By a Russian Officer*, London, 1813.

Bennigsen, General Count Levin August Théophil, *Mémoires du général Bennigsen*, 3 vols, Paris, 1907–08. (Chief of Staff, Russian Headquarters)

Chichagov, Admiral Pavel, *Mémoires de l'Amiral Tchichagoff (1767–1849)*, Leipzig, 1862. (Commanding Army of the Danube)

Clausewitz, Karl von, *Feldzug 1812 in Russland, from Hinterlassene Werke uber krieg und kriegfuhrung*, Berlin, 1832–37. Translated as *The Campaign of 1812 in Russia*, London, 1843 and 1992. (Attached to Russian Headquarters)

Crossard, Baron de, *Mémoires militaires et historiques pour servir a l'histoire de la guerre depuis 1792 jusqu'en 1815 inclusivement*, Paris, 1829.

Damas, Ange Hyacinthe Maxence, *Mémoires du Baron de Damas (1785–1862)*, 2 vols, Paris, 1922.

Davidov, Denis, *In the Service of the Tsar against Napoleon: The Memoirs of Denis Davidov, 1806–14*, London, 1999. (Akhtyrka Hussars, later partisan leader)

Durova, Nadezhda, *The Cavalry Maiden*, London, 1988. (Lithuanian Uhlans, 4th Cavalry Division, IV Cavalry Corps)

Ermolov, A. P., *Zapiski A. P. Ermolova, 1798–1826*, Moscow, 1991. (First Army of the West)

Glinka, Fyodor Nikolayevitch, *Pisma russkogo offitsera*, Moscow, 1987. (ADC to General Miloradovich, First Army of the West)

Golitzyn, Nikolai Borisovich, *Souvenirs et impressions d'un officier Russe pendant les campagnes de 1812, 1813 et 1814*, St Petersburg, 1849.

Langeron, Général, *Mémoires de Langeron, général d'infanterie dans l'armée russe: Campagnes de 1812, 1813, 1814*, Paris, 1902. (I Corps, Army of the Danube)

Löwenstern, Eduard von, *Mit Graf Pahlens Reiterei gegen Napoleon. Denkwüdigkeiten des russischen Generals Eduard von Löwenstern (1790–1827)*, Berlin, 1907. (ADC to General Pahlen, 3rd Cavalry Division, First Army of the West)

Löwenstern, Woldemar Hermann, Baron von, *Mémoires du général-major Baron de Löwenstern (1776–1858)*, 2 vols, Paris, 1903. (ADC to Barclay de Tolly, First Army of the West)

Martens, Carl von, *Denkwüdigkeiten aus dem leben eines alten offiziers*, Dresden, 1848. (Izyumskii Hussars, 2nd Division, IV Corps)

Mitarevskii, Nikolai, Evstafievich, *Vospominaniya o voine 1812 goda*, Moscow, 1871. (12th Light Artillery Company, 7th Infantry Division, VI Corps)

Pisarev, Aleksandr, *Voennaia Pis'ma*, 2 vols, Moscow, 1817. (Semenovskii Guard Regiment, Guard Division, V Corps)

Pokhvisnev, Ivan, *Zhurnal ili zapiski voiny otkrytoi Franzusami v Rossiji 1812 g*, 2 vols, Moscow, 1830–33. (2nd Ukrainian Cossacks)

Rochechouart, Louis Victor Léon, *Souvenirs sur la Révolution, l'Empire et la Restauration*, Paris, 1889. (Serving with the Army of the Danube)

Rodozhitskii, Ilya Timofeyovitch, *Pokhodnye zapiski artillerista, s 1812 po 1816 god*, Moscow, 1835. (3rd Light Artillery Company, 11th Infantry Division, II Corps)

Schubert, F. von, *Unter dem doppeladler: Erinnerungen eines Deutschen im Russischen Offiziersdienst, 1789–1814*, Stuttgart, 1962. (ADC to Barclay de Tolly, First Army of the West)

Tchicherin, Aleksander Vasilevich, *Dnevnik Aleksandra Tchicherina, 1812–1813*, Moscow, 1966. (Semenovskii Guard Regiment, Guard Division, V Corps)

Toll, General von der, *Denkwüdigkeiten des russischen Generals von der Toll*, 2 vols, Leipzig, 1856. (Quartermaster General, Russian Headquarters)

Uxküll, Baron Boris, *Arms and the Woman: The Diaries of Baron Boris Uxküll, 1812–1819*, London, 1966.

Vyasjemsskij, Prince P., *Vospominaniya o 1812 g*, Moscow, 1869. (ADC to General Miloradovich, First Army of the West)

Wickede, Julius von, *Wider Napoleon! Ein deutsches Reiterleben, 1806–1815*, 2 vols, Stuttgart, 1911.

Wilson, Sir Robert, *Private Diary of Travels, Personal Services, and Public Events, during Mission and Employment with the European Armies in the Campaigns of 1812, 1813 and 1814, from the Invasion of Russia to the Capture of Paris*, 2 vols, London, 1861. Also *General Wilson's Journal, 1812–14*, London, 1964. (British liaison officer at Russian Headquarters)

Wolzogen, Ludwig, *Memorien des kongl. preuss. Generals Ludwig Freiherrn von Wolzogen*, Leipzig, 1851. (Staff, First Army of the West)

Württemberg, Eugen von, *Erinnerungen aus dem Feldzuge des Jahres 1812 in Russland von dem Herzog Eugen von Württemberg*, Breslau, 1846. (Commanded 4th Division, II Corps)

Zotov, R., *Rasskazy o pokhodakh 1812 i 1813 godov praporschika sanktpeterburgskogo opoltcheniya*, St Petersburg, 1836. (14th Battalion, St Petersburg Militia, I Corps)

Journals

Andreyev, Nikolai Ivanovich, 'Vospominaniya', *Russki Archiv*, 1879, Book III. (50th Jäger Regiment, 27th Infantry Division, VII Corps)

Maievski, 'Vospominaniya', *Antiquités Russes*, 1873. (Russian Headquarters)

Tiedemann, Oberstleutnant von, 'Tagebuch und Briefwechsel des Oberstleutnants v. T. aus dem Jahre 1812', *Jahrbuch f. d. deutsche Armee und Marine*, Bd 24.